THE GLADIATOR MINDSET

Adam Peaty

Written with Richard Waters

Quercus

First published in Great Britain in 2021 by

Quercus Editions Ltd
Carmelite House
50 Victoria Embankment
London EC4Y 0DZ

An Hachette UK company

A CIP catalogue record for this book is available
from the British Library

HB ISBN 978 1 52941 842 2
TPB ISBN 978 1 52941 843 9
Ebook ISBN 978 1 52941 844 6

10 9 8 7 6 5 4 3

Typeset by CC Book Production
Printed and bound in Great Britain by Clays Ltd, Elcograf S.p.A.

Papers used by Quercus Editions Ltd. are from well-managed forests
and other responsible sources.

*For George – I hope this book will guide you
and give you wisdom through your life*

Contents

The Gladiator Mindset

Me and Mel a few moments after receiving my first Olympic Gold in a world record time.

Introduction

There are certain moments in my life that stick out as more unforgettable than others, like winning my first Olympic gold medal and the birth of my son George. But I believe it's what you do every single day in the present that defines you: the little kindnesses, doing things properly without cutting corners, treating people with respect, being honest and straight up . . . putting your best self forward. I look back on my life so far and realise everything has a ripple effect upon everything else.

I'll give you an example. My first swimming club was Dove Valley where I trained with a pal called Kyle whose mum worked for a mortgage company. She happened to meet a lady called Mel Marshall while organising her house purchase. Mel, a former world champion and twice Olympian, told her she was a swimming coach and asked her to bring her son to Derby Swimming Club if he wanted to come. I went along to keep Kyle company, and it was here in 2014 that I was *discovered*. This was a major turning point, as Mel instantly saw the potential in my breaststroke. Apparently, she thought, 'Bloody hell, he looks like a JCB eating up the water!' Since that fateful day, she has taught me pretty much everything I know about swimming, and to a certain extent, life. Little did I know that in the years that followed she would have such a powerful and charismatic effect on me through her continuous and undivided mentorship.

But for all that she's given me, none of it would have been worth a penny without my appetite to succeed and absorb what was taught to me. It was my mindset and her constant wisdom and encouragement that got me through, and just as Mel taught me to flow with water rather than going against it, my approach has allowed me not to get stuck but to keep flowing forward. She likes to say, 'There's not a strand of DNA in that boy that I haven't had a hand in.' On all those endless journeys back from the pool when we were stuck in traffic, Mel would use the time to teach me how to reframe my teenage anger and make it work for me rather than against me.

The mind is the engine that drives the body, the general that commands the foot soldier, and it's my belief that if we are committed and willing to making the necessary personal investments, we are all capable of locating greatness within us and achieving the impossible. Whether you are old and wise or young and bursting with energy, there are limits you are imposing on yourself that this book will help you reconsider. Perhaps you think you are over the hill, your last chance at doing a triathlon is behind you, or maybe when you look in the mirror you only see the bits of yourself that you're not happy with. I'm here to tell you it isn't over yet, not by a long way. That if you can find what you love doing and then apply yourself to it you will be surprised just how much you can achieve and how enjoyable it is. People talk about the sacrifices I made and how many times I turned down going clubbing or to the pub when I was growing up as a young teenage swimmer because I was constantly training. It wasn't really a sacrifice, it was a choice. My Olympic gold medal warms my insides when it sits polished and pristine in the palm of my hand. Nothing comes without hard work – you just need the discipline and consistency to execute it. I can promise achieving your most cherished goal will not be a piece of cake; if it was that accessible it wouldn't be worth striving for. But if you are armed with positivity and have good people around you, a bullet-proof purpose and the inner determination to realise your goal through hard work and discipline, you're already well on your way.

My mum and dad are working-class parents and I have two older brothers and one older sister. As the youngest I was the go-to punchbag and constantly had to prove myself; it helped that I was naturally extremely competitive (if I wasn't winning at Monopoly then no one else was going to either – I'd swipe the board!). I've since learnt how to lose gracefully, though it doesn't happen often! Addictive natures (and occasionally, sporting prowess) run deep in the current of my family's DNA. My uncle John Peaty was a professional boxer in the stable of legendary bare-knuckle fighter and Gypsy King, Bartley Gorman (a relative of Tyson Fury), while another of my uncles suffered with his own demons.

Growing up in my household there were a few behavioural challenges among my siblings, but despite the chaos I wanted to work even harder. I haven't been diagnosed with anything specific but for certain I'm somewhere on the spectrum, as my mind is better able to focus when I'm moving or exercising. Adversity is the fire on which the blade of ambition is forged, so rather than leave home and find somewhere else to live, I decided to stay and keep myself to myself. We all walk a genetic razor-blade of hardwired hereditary flaws, I've always tried to make sure my considerable energy is channelled into something positive.

My spirit is fed by swimming and inspiring other people. I want to share my story with you so next time you see me on the blocks at the Olympics you can understand who I am, why I do what I do and where I've come from; the obstacles I faced in my life and how I used them to motivate myself rather than pull me down. If I can get through all that and prevail, then so can you.

This book focuses on the transformative processes that have helped me – and continue to do so – in my pursuit of unprecedented excellence. It will teach you the benefits of pushing yourself beyond your known limits during training so that, cometh the hour, you are ready to perform at your optimum level, whatever's thrown at you – even if it's your trunks splitting ten minutes before a championship-level race! I'll show you that you have so much more in your tank than you realise, be it grit, oxygen or reserves of endurance. All of this is waiting for you to access it. We'll look at how to process pain through developing a gladiator's mindset, plus the vital need for clarity of purpose in your everyday life. We'll talk about how you can get in flow with yourself so training can become a joy, and how to channel anger for positive purposes as well as getting to know different kinds of fatigue that may be holding you back. I'll also share my diet and training secrets with you.

Additionally, at the end of most chapters you'll find a straightforward exercise designed to help you put into practice and embed some of my mental and physical techniques. I hope this book inspires you to find and develop your talent and have the confidence to believe in yourself. Let's all be better than we were yesterday, shall we? Time to attack!

Adam Peaty, August 2021

Prologue

Gunning for Gold

A younger version of myself racing at Staffordshire County Championships, 2007.

Rio Olympics, 8 August 2016

We wait in the ready room for our names to be called before our individual walk to the blocks. It's like that scene in Ridley Scott's *Gladiator* when Maximus is waiting in the dark corridor before the portcullis lifts and the gladiators spill onto the sand of the arena, blinking like moles in the brilliant sunlight. Each of us Olympians is lost in thought. I've fought my way through periods of self-doubt and physical punishment to be stood where I am, and finally it is happening, I'm here where I always planned to be, to win the most coveted prize an athlete can ever hope for, an Olympic gold.

The swimmer in front walks off as his name is called. Me next.

'Ad-a-am ... Pe-a-ty!' thunders a voice overhead.

Let's get ready to rumble! I think as I lift my chin, breathe deep, relax my shoulders and roll my neck muscles. The night smells of excitement, opportunity and chlorine. The crowd roars and I walk slowly to my lane and peel off my navy tracksuit, keeping on my goggles and a blood-red swimming cap. Thousands of people are sitting in the swimming arena watching this race. Across the world, over multiple time zones – from Loughborough to Lagos – over twenty-seven million are tuned in to watch the 2016 Rio Olympics, and many more will watch it far into the future. My stomach is fluttering with pigeon-sized butterflies as I step up onto the blocks for the men's final of the 100m breaststroke, but I am fully in control. I'm in lane four and to my immediate right is my arch-rival and the reigning Olympic champion, Cameron van der Burgh, who also beat me a few times during his career. Cody Miller, the American, is to my left in lane three.

I feel as if my life has been building towards this single moment: the 4 a.m mornings before dawn when normal people were asleep and I was swimming up and down a pool, so tired on occasions my eyes were shut; the trying not to fall asleep in class; the diets, the muscle building, the struggle to become a professional athlete complicated by my often dysfunctional domestic life; the sacrifices others have made to get me here, their investment of time and belief in me; my ups and downs . . . But here I am, twenty-one years old and racing the finest in the world in this, the biggest moment of my life. No wonder my heart's thumping, my body coursing with adrenaline and I'm covered head to foot in goosebumps.

It's hard to believe I'm in Rio, living in the Olympic village in the company of sporting giants, bumping into living legends like Michael Phelps. This morning, as I left my room with my kitbag and headed for the pool, I said to myself, 'Either you're going to return to this room as the new Olympic champion and world record holder or as a silver medallist. Weird as it may seem to some of you readers, I quite enjoyed putting that pressure on myself. Sometimes you've got to give yourself an ultimatum.

As I climb on a bus it's 10 p.m. in the village, the humid air mercifully fresh tonight with an offshore breeze. I'm racing at one o'clock in the morning; there's plenty of time to put my war-face on and get myself amped up and ready for battle. I feel present, my senses hyper-aware of my Brazilian surroundings – the chatter of other athletes around me in a babel of accents – the whole experience is intoxicating. It's a twenty-minute ride to the Olympic Aquatics Stadium in the Barra Olympic Park. I listen to my chilled Olympic Games playlist to distract myself from my thoughts. Music plays a special role for me in high-performance situations.

The Olympic Park, for all the salivating and doom-mongering of the international press claiming that it wouldn't be built in time, looks terrific. Despite Brazil's ongoing Zika virus epidemic, the Russian doping scandal and the diving pool turning bogey-green, the Olympic Games, first staged in 776 BC, prevail. The Aquatics Stadium is a vast, naturally ventilated rectangular building with a thin PVC membrane draped over a steel-framed roof. Lit in purple neon and perched upon the edge of a lagoon, it looks spectacularly futuristic. Inside, athletes are already racing and warming up. This is where I begin my usual prep: fifteen minutes relaxing, chatting to the physio; stretching, warm-up on land, then another hour in the practice pool. There are four pools here for swimmers: two in the Olympic village, and two in the Aquatics Stadium; an outdoor warm-up pool behind the main Olympic pool itself.

I spot the willowy form of Michael Phelps and pass in the slipstream of his legend, thinking, 'I'm going to be like you one day.' Some people say you should never meet your heroes, but I reckon I'll make an exception for him. His presence is electric, and as he moves the other Olympians part to let him pass and hang off his every expression.

I may be the current world champion but it means nothing compared to being the Olympic champion. The mythic appeal of these Games dates back thousands of years to the Greek Peloponnese and classical Greece. The sense of heritage is like no other: Muhammad Ali, as a young skinny Cassius Clay, won an Olympic gold, as did Mike Tyson. And then in the pool there was Mark Spitz, Ian Thorpe and of course the majestic Phelps. Even Hercules was said to have competed in the ancient Greek Olympics.

Representing your country is a proud moment for any athlete, but the absolute pinnacle for any sportsperson is to do so at the Olympics – the Mount Olympus of all competitions, that rarefied place up in the clouds where athletes for a brief moment can become gods and forever be remembered for their achievements. The preparation each of us has had to go through to be here is brutal and hopefully worth all the pain, but it's a gamble; tragedy and triumph are waiting in the wings for all who compete, and they have only one or two chances to prove themselves worthy of the illustrious gold medal.

Back on the blocks, the noise becomes almost deafening and, as my heartbeat quickens, I try and remain calm and composed. 'Everything will go to plan,' I tell myself. 'You're as ready as you'll ever be.' Red, white and blue GB flags flutter in the audience as my nerves vanish, replaced by a steeliness and a cold, hard voice inside me that tells me this is my moment, I'm as fit as a butcher's dog and what I may lack in years I make up for with determination and grit. I love the Union Jack and I love my country and I'm going to fight like hell for it. Anger is no stranger to me, and with the help of my coach and mentor Mel Marshall I have learnt to make friends with it.

Yes, it was good to break the 100m breaststroke world record in the heats yesterday, but I'm just getting started . . . A whistle sounds, the crowd hushes to a murmur, then another whistle shrieks to alert the finalists to get in the start position. 'Gentlemen, take your marks.' In that instant it's as if time slows down, the muscled and sinewy bodies tensing around me, I'm just hungry to get in the water. The starting bleeper finally sounds and as I propel myself off the blocks with a good start – not something I can always claim – for a moment I and the other swimmers are airborne in deadly silence. We pierce the water in unison, maximising our single kick and underwater pull before surfacing to an almighty cheer from the crowd. As I bob up and down, one second I hear them, the next everything is muted as I submerge.

I'm attacking the water with clean strokes, my mind and body in harmony, my stroke and breathing perfect, balancing speed and aggression, technique and emotion. I'm leading at the turn – in swimming we call it 'the back end' – and heading into the final straight I begin to stretch my lead from neck-and-neck to total domination. My body feels like it could go for ever as I touch the wall and in doing so I look under my arm for Cameron van der Burgh, but he's not there, no one is. Hard to believe but I've not only won by a body length and prevailed on the biggest stage of all, I've also completely dominated the event!

The crowd roars as a new world record flashes up on the board. I've smashed the WR I set earlier this week in the heats, beating it by four-tenths of a second, and it's a second and a half quicker than the last Olympic Games. I came to Rio to set a new standard and master my events, and the feeling of fulfilling this goal is beyond special. Yep, I'm just getting started.

Chapter One

Limitless – Project 56 and Project Immortal

Start of the 2020 season: little did I know it would be delayed a whole year!

have a saying that I try to live by: 'Always be better than yesterday.' Anybody whose desire is to be the best at what they do has to be obsessed with self-improvement. Every day I ask myself, 'Is this meal or workout going to make me faster? Does it fit in with my purpose? If not, I liaise with Mel and hopefully bin it. That level of single-mindedness might sound a bit over the top, but if I'm to continue breaking records it has to be this way. And time is precious, I'm twenty-six now and won't be swimming forever, so I want to pack in all that I can, to shoot for the stars and achieve the impossible.

Impossible is just a concept

Impossible. A ten-letter word – that's all it is – and yet it has such a negative hold on us. Maybe it would serve society better if we were to remove it from our dictionaries! As we'll see throughout this book, success is about the quality of the messages you feed your mind – that and giving yourself permission to be great, and wanting it so badly you can almost reach out and touch it. Just because something has not been done before it doesn't mean that it's impossible. When Frank Jarvis, winner of the men's 100m at the 1900 Olympics, clocked 11.0 seconds, it was considered a miracle, but today that time would not even qualify him for a spot in the junior nationals. Never say never.

A few years ago, the prospect of going to Mars was a science fiction writer's daydream until Elon Musk, the originator of PayPal and Tesla, appeared on the can-do horizon. Musk uses a method of thinking called 'first principles' to solve problems: the process of stripping back how something works, reverse-engineering it to the basics and a stage where you understand it perfectly. From this base of certainty, you gradually work forward to resolve the problem.

The problem in question was the sheer distance to Mars, a minimum seven-month journey, the sheer expense and the fact there was no known craft capable of landing in the Martian environment and taking off again to return to Earth. 'Impossible!' crowed the establishment. But the inventor, despite all the naysayers and multiple failed attempts at landing said rocket on pontoons in the sea, successfully pioneered a working rocket that could fulfil all the technical requirements. SpaceX has made the impossible possible. All this from a man who was ridiculed for his sky-high ambition. Musk's newest company, Neuralink, is developing artificially intelligent microchips that can be inserted in the brains of paraplegics and will enable them to walk again. Even amputees will soon be able to adapt and fully control bionic limbs with their mind. Whoever would have dreamt this? Musk did, then he put in eighty-hour weeks to make it happen.

Society creates boundaries but mavericks break them down

Just as it creates rules designed to police and protect us, society also creates limits that hold us back; safe, formulaic, predictable paths that see you go to school, then high school, on to university and then you get a job and buy a house. I threw the rule book out of the window when I was fifteen, leaving education to pursue my professional sporting career. I knew I had to do something outrageous and unique to put my stamp on the world. Society tells us how to behave, and what is or isn't achievable. Sometimes it's out of date and needs to change. Lately we have been telling society how it should behave and it's being rebooted with a much-needed update.

I love stories about mavericks, freethinkers and rebels – people who go their own way, flick their middle finger at the status quo and demonstrate that 'impossible' is just a negative word. Consider Captain Matthew Webb, who in

1875 – covered in porpoise fat and dressed in a woollen bathing suit – became the first person to swim the English Channel, despite it being considered at the time far too rough, the currents too powerful. Think of the polar explorer Ranulph Fiennes who, at sixty-five, became the oldest Briton to successfully scale Everest in 2009. It wasn't just his age that was against him: mentally, he had a lifelong fear of heights, and physically, he was missing the tips of his thumb and all the fingers on his left hand (after he returned from the Arctic with frostbite and sawed them off), not to mention his dodgy heart. But contrary to the naysayers, after two failed attempts Fiennes made it to the summit of the world's highest mountain.

In my life I have constantly been thrown challenges, and being a pioneer in my sport has been the hardest; stripping my stroke down to the bare basics and building it back up into something that worked. I was often told that there was no future in being a sportsperson, yet what other job would have me travelling the world learning about new cultures and racing against the best of the best?

Who says you can't be a great achiever?

The history books are bursting with amazing achievements that were previously considered unachievable. We are constantly rewriting popular wisdom on what can and can't be done, proving we can always get quicker, fitter, stronger . . .

better. Who is to say you can't be one of these achievers? In 2006 comedian David Walliams swam the English Channel in ten hours and thirty-four minutes to become the 666th person to complete the challenge, with the 48th quickest time in history. He wasn't a natural swimmer, he just applied himself. In 2009, Eddie Izzard, the stand-up comedian and actor, announced he was going to run forty-three marathons in fifty-one days, with only five weeks' training. 'That's insane,' people said. 'He'll never do it – you need a minimum four months' training to attempt even a single marathon.' And yet Eddie achieved his goal.

I'm ultra-competitive. I've always believed I can go faster and that I have the capability to push through new boundaries. My original goal to swim sub-58 seconds in the 100m breaststroke I achieved when I won gold in Rio at the 2016 Olympics, smashing my existing world record of 57.92 seconds with a new time of 57.13 seconds. Up until then no one had thought it possible to swim a sub-58, but I knew I was just getting warmed up.

'Project 56' became my new Everest. And at the 2019 World Aquatics Championships in Gwangju, South Korea I became the first ever human to swim the 100m breaststroke sub-57 seconds, with a winning time of 56.88 seconds and a gap of 1.4 seconds between myself and the next swimmer. Once you're at the top of your chosen profession you've got to keep that spot. I've been the world's quickest breaststroke swimmer for seven years now, with only one loss.

Just as I was inspired by the great Kosuke Kitajima, Japan's unbeatable breaststroker, the thought that I am inspiring future generations of swimmers is a very powerful one to have in my mind.

I don't believe in going to a championship saying: 'I'm here to defend my title.' It makes no sense – it's a different competition in a different year, a different moment in time in a different country. In Rio I was racing for myself and my family. That hasn't changed but now I am racing for my son and my girlfriend Eiri too, which is ten times more powerful. When I tap my chest twice before the race it is for them both.

People say: 'The only place you can go from the top is down.' I say there's another option: you continue pushing upwards, look forward not back, and never focus on your competitors, just yourself. Like the personal best ghost in a video game, I'm essentially racing against myself now in my pursuit of new world records. The greatest conquerors and adventurers in history didn't stop – they kept on going, hungry to achieve their ultimate goal. And then they slept! I'll sleep when I'm dead or content – either of them are equally dangerous to me – and for a very long time. In the meantime, life is there to be grabbed by the balls.

The obstacle is the way

You've got to create a process (game plan or system) that serves your purpose and which you can stick to. By doing so you'll eventually achieve your 'impossible', overcoming impediments like the recent pandemic and navigating whatever else the universe throws at you. The Stoics of ancient Greece and Rome believed 'the obstacle is the way', and by way of explanation told a story of a king who wanted to measure the resilience of his people, so he placed a huge boulder blocking the road that led to his city. It was inconvenient and caused a backlog of angry traders trying to get through the city gates to sell their wares. Some argued with each other while some turned tail and left it to a sharper mind to figure a way past the boulder. One man perceived the obstacle not as an impossibility but rather as a challenge – something he could grow from if he figured it out. Having moved the rock, he discovered a pot of gold beneath it. The moral of the story is that if you look for positives in a negative situation, rather than just focusing on the negative, you can prosper from it and learn about yourself.

Lockdown allowed me to take a bit of a mental break from the rigours of professional swimming. With the pandemic spreading and pools shut, training in a pool was out of my hands, but I was of the mindset that something positive could be taken from it, so I focused on lifting weights in the garage and cycling. It also gave me more time to relax with Eiri while she was pregnant; not many know this but we had barely known each other when lockdown occurred and we received the fantastic but scary news that we were going to become parents. I remember Eiri crying on the phone as she broke the news to me, at the time I was in a high-intensive training camp in Australia. It hit me hard in more ways than one, but from that day forward my life changed irreversibly. And for the better.

Despite not being able to train in my usual way during lockdown, as well as getting ill and becoming a dad, in 2020 I managed to break my twelfth and thirteenth world record. If you *really* want something in life, be it a gold medal, a promotion, to climb a mountain, fulfil an ambition or create a legacy that you hope will never be forgotten, you must find the *purpose* in yourself which will drive you to meet the demands required to attain it, whatever boulders you might run into on the way. A short and simple quote I use when I'm tired and unmotivated is: 'Ninety percent of success is just showing up.'

Recently, I've been working on my start off the blocks, which has always been my Achilles heel, and it's improved by a second in the first 15 metres, and that's just 15 per cent of the race! If I can find that in just 15 metres, what else can I find in the remaining 85? In my vocabulary there is no such thing as defence, only attack. You're here to fight, to push your body and mind further than they are *supposed* to go. Hard work is ingrained in me. I love training because it gives me the chance to strive and prosper.

I believe that if you can clearly picture your own success, then you can achieve it. The mind needs to be fed with positive, specific and repetitive images so it knows exactly what is expected of it. This is what I did before the Tokyo Olympics. Doubt is not a welcome guest in the champion's mindset. It's the way in which we think that defines what we do and how well we do it, be it as people or athletes. A close friend of mine says: 'If you're not incredibly excited by your goal it's not worth pursuing.' As a competitor, while I respect those competitors on the blocks next to me I'm also aware they are the only ones who stand before me and my goal. Everyone suffers a loss at some time or other, mainly through variables they cannot control, so I say: 'Control the controllables, don't try and control the uncontrollables.'

Tell yourself you're going to be a champion enough times and you start to believe it

Ross Edgley, the respected sports scientist and athlete-adventurer who made a name for himself by swimming around Great Britain tied to a log (yes, you read that correctly!), believes that, physiologically speaking, each one of us is 'biologically unique'. He also asserts: 'We still don't fully know what the human body is capable of, so why limit it?' Edgley goes on to say that when we put ourselves under exceptional physical strain, 'a range of dormant genes in the DNA are expressed and extraordinary physiological

27

processes are activated.' In other words, we blossom under adversity: it is in this very place of conflict between stasis and disruption that the magic happens, and our bodies adapt and evolve. The psychiatrist Carl Jung once said, 'I am what I choose to become.' We can be *whoever* we wish to be and achieve *whatever* we desire, so long as our mind fully accepts and believes it. In truth your mind will pretty much support anything you tell it, and if there is a disconnect between where/who you are and where/who you want to be, your mind will try and bridge the gap. We call this the 'law of attraction'.

Ever since he was a boy, Tyson Fury always told everyone he was going to be the world heavyweight boxing champion, as did Muhammad Ali (then Cassius Clay). Are you beginning to see the pattern? You say something enough times and your mind and body begin to work in concert towards that goal. The greatest enemy of positive change is the comfort zone. Comfort zones are the killers of progress and ambition. If you want to achieve something really special it's not good enough to just turn up for life, you need to push yourself to where you've never been, and that involves change and disruption. Remember, Einstein said: 'If you always do what you've always done, you'll always get what you've always got.'

Obviously, there may be physical limits to how fast I can swim and how much endurance training I can sustain, but I don't think about them. If I did I wouldn't have succeeded in producing the twenty quickest breaststroke times in history or breaking fourteen world records, as those limiting thoughts would have sabotaged my sense of possibility. There's another old saying that 'Everything moves from the head down', meaning the body follows the directions of the brain. I completely agree with this: our mind is the control room and arbiter of all our triumphs and failures. Keeping the mind engaged and on track with what you want is paramount and takes practice; given the chance, your mind will always take the easy route and make excuses for not pushing yourself, and it can sound very convincing. According to former SBS soldier turned TV presenter, Ant Middleton: 'You can't trust your body. It tells you you've got nothing left when it's still a hundred miles from breaking. The only true war you'll ever fight is with your own mind.'

Your mind carries your body. You need to constantly ensure everything is right in your head before you can expect your body to perform. Ask yourself: 'Am I happy? Healthy? Have I prepared sufficiently for this challenge? What else can I do to make sure I'm primed to win? Do I need a break before I push on? When you're running the last 50 metres of a 400m race and your legs start to wobble, it's your brain that will ultimately decide whether you give in to the lactic acid filling your legs or push on to win. Two choices: quit and accept defeat; or take the pain, remember it's only temporary, and push through. Scientists dedicate their careers to researching why the body performs as it does at breaking point, but if we're not careful we can become victims of 'paralysis by analysis', trying to digest every inch of data when we're not performing. All I need to know is when to push and when to relax. Sometimes simplicity wins.

Most days I get up and my body is trashed from training so hard. It feels broken and sore and tells me I can't do any more. But then I remind myself to get into the rhythm of things and realise that all I need to do is be in a positive mindset, one that considers everything as achievable. If you can separate your thought process from being tired but remain positive in your mind, there is no limit to where you can take your brain and mindset.

The brain is a weapon

To pursue success – be it to get fitter, stronger or quicker – you need to be able to separate the body from the mind. David Goggins, former US Navy Seal, ultramarathon runner and holder of the world record for doing four thousand pull-ups in seventeen hours, says in his book, *Can't Hurt Me*, 'Your brain is the most powerful weapon in the world. It is talking to you in all different kinds of ways, and it wants to control you . . . [so] you've got to tell your brain where you want it to go and how you want to get there.' Goggins describes his first battle with the 'control room' in his head and how he gave himself no way out. His mind, having had a stern talking to, said, 'Okay, we're going to adapt and overcome now.'

*

Darren Hardy is someone I admire. He's a gentle Northern Irishman and former soldier turned altruist, ultrarunner and endurance athlete. And, last but not least, a master of breaking through pain barriers. Following his tour of duty during the Iraq war he now suffers from PTSD (post-traumatic stress disorder). When a British Lynx helicopter was shot down in Basra, Hardy and his colleagues had to secure a very 'hot' hostile area to pick up the pieces of the downed airmen's bodies. He believes this was the cause of his trauma, but it wasn't triggered until years later when Hardy saved a girl who was trapped in a fire in Canada. That same scent of burning skin was what brought it all back to him. After fifteen years' service in the British Army, he was discharged on medical grounds. In 2018, Hardy was ready to pull the pin on life but for the fact that he had two young daughters that needed a father. As a former physical trainer in the army, he believed his salvation lay in exercise, and for the last three years he has taken on a series of challenges that many would think foolhardy, in order to keep himself sane and to raise money for worthy causes. 'My driver is to show people that if you put your mind to something anything is possible.'

He's run five marathons back to back; completed seven Iron Man competitions in a row; competed in the 480-kilometre Montane Yukon Arctic Ultra run and many more. His next adventure is to be the first man to complete an Iron Man in the most northerly place yet, the island of Svalbard in the Arctic Circle (where the polar bear population outnumbers the few humans who can live in this extreme place). He has a stocky, muscular rugby player's body which more lends itself to short, explosive bursts of energy like sprinting rather than long distances. And yet, with little training and by sheer force of will, he is able to run incredible distances due to his ability to switch off his mind to pain and fatigue.

We are all capable of greatness. Don't be scared of your potential for brilliance – the only ceiling you have above you is the one you or others have built for yourself. To be great you have to quieten your inner critic, get into the habit of telling your mind who is boss and learn to slow its manic thoughts right down. And to do that you need to develop trust and self-respect.

Step 1: Imagine you are the hero in your own movie

What would you give yourself permission to attempt which you don't in ordinary life? Think of something you would love to do, as if there were no obstacles in front of you stopping you achieving it. How would your hero go about it, what would he need to do to make it happen? Create the scenario in as much detail as possible and write it all down so you can read it through and keep refining it. Make a note of why it would be worth attempting and how it would make you feel. The more challenging the better. Also be aware that this is a game, so hush the voice that immediately questions you and says it's impossible. Maybe you imagine yourself to be an award-winning actor, or CEO of a company you've built from nothing; maybe your hero gets themselves in amazing shape or becomes multi-lingual ... The possibilities are endless if you only allow your imagination to get past the fog of self-limitation. Remember it's your hero, not you ... at least not yet!

Chapter Two

Identifying Your Inner Purpose and Creating Your Goals

At Victoria Falls in Zambia, 2012. We cycled 500km for charity.

This book is about changing your thinking and some of your default behaviours in order to reach your goals and maximise your potential. It's also about finding your true purpose, which is the reason for wanting to reach your goals in the first place. Your purpose is, in essence, your mission in life, the reason you're on planet Earth. A person without purpose is a person without a sense of meaning; they feel alienated, like a leaf drifting listlessly on a wide ocean. People are at their happiest when they have a reason *why* they are doing what they are doing; this then becomes striving. Without such a reason it becomes toil. It doesn't matter how old you are, if you don't find a purpose your life will lack substance and every day will be the same. This is why some people get depressed when they retire (particularly men) as they are overly defined by their work and when that stops and they're no longer achieving, crisis hits. At the opposite end of the timeline adolescents often derail because they have all this energy but no sense of purpose to channel it towards.

Aspire or spiral

We thrive on momentum, when we are involved in the *doing* – going, making, building, solving, developing … Ever since our ancestors stopped flicking shit at one another in the trees, waved goodbye to the other primates and left to see what was on the other side of the distant ridge, we have been an active species. Without activity we become depressed and stagnant, and we spiral downwards. It's in our DNA to reach for the stars, and having reached them to be curious about then getting to the next cluster of stars. We should allow ourselves the pleasure of enjoying the challenge, acceptant in the knowledge that part of us is going to be forever restless, but we should celebrate ambition and achievement, knowing we are living to our full potential.

Pleasure is only found in the challenge if it's a challenge we consider important to us, a task that gets all our neurons flashing, engages our skills and perhaps involves learning new ones in order to complete it. Karl Marx once said, 'Teach a man to fish, but the fishes he catches aren't his, they belong to the person paying him to fish …' If we're busting our ass working for 'the man', stuck to the same repetitious task where there is no sense of achievement and no requirement for original creative thought, we just switch off. Some call this the computer mode. It's as if we are asleep.

Every season I sit down with my most trusted members of the British Swimming team to create an IAP or Individual Athlete Plan. This is the foundation of what I want to achieve throughout the coming year, and comprises all the small goals I need to reach in order to achieve success at the championships. The idea of the IAP is to get faster but I use it to keep things fresh so I don't become a victim of stagnation. Going from 2018 into 2019, I knew I had to switch my mindset and work ethic up a notch. I had beaten my world record by three one hundredths of a second at the European Championships, but this didn't feed the beast inside of me whose sole purpose is to strive further and further.

I train in a relatively large group, but we work out either individually or as part of a smaller group in order for the feedback to become more personal and tailored. It's no surprise that some people we work with every day are going to piss us off, that's just life, but going into the next year this would be an area where I could improve. Patience, tolerance and understanding that others are on a different journey would be part of my personal improvement. In response to how I could better my environment so my purpose could flourish, I remember saying quite pointedly, 'I can't be arsed with toxicity, I have no time or energy for it.'

Whether we're painting a portrait, building a house or forming a company, we were born to be creative, to think our way around problems, and when this spark dies, part of us does too. Rapidly. When we just turn up for work, clock in, switch off for eight hours then clock out for the day, we feel diminished and cheated. The man who catches fish to feed his family, or to sell to others to feed his family, is much happier because he understands *why* he is doing it – there's a purpose. And in the doing of it he ennobles himself.

Part of us, in a very ancient quarter of our collective memory, celebrates the great things we have achieved as a species, deeds we should be fiercely proud of: mastering fire, flight, going to space; the creation of music; establishing democracy; proving the world is round ... mapping our world and the galaxy in which it sits; finding vaccines. In the remembering of these great endeavours there's a spark that lights up in all of us which would love to be a contributor to this litany of triumph, and knows it has the capacity for greatness. We need to keep moving, learning and evolving, and purpose is the super fuel that drives us forward to realise the impossible.

When we allow ourselves to be blown through life like flotsam, we feel lazy, torpid, frustrated and unfulfilled. It's as if we're missing a part of a jigsaw, leading to anxiety and unhappiness. This is because our naturally active nature has been neglected or become blocked and is trying to get back out. We feel at our best when we're challenged and prevail despite the obstacles along the way; when we imagine and then realise something which matters to us and we know *why* we're doing it.

Two guys cleaning a beach of litter, both doing exactly the same task – one is happy and the other is bored. Why? Because one of them is a passionate environmentalist, and every empty can and discarded nappy he picks up is contributing incrementally to a healthier planet. He has a purpose. The other guy is just doing a job for which he feels nothing, and has no investment in what he's doing – he's just marking time.

Old wisdom

One day I'd like to go to university and study classics. You'll have guessed by looking at my tats that I have a love for the ancient world, especially the ancient Greeks and Romans, and much of their wisdom will pepper these pages. The ink work on my arms is a reminder to me of the principles I live by: the lion represents courage and England, who I am proud to race for; the goddess Athena is for wisdom; Achilles for fearlessness; the word 'Equilibrium' is to remind me to take time out to reset and enjoy the present– what's the point of getting to your destination if you didn't enjoy the journey? There's also a Spartan soldier to represent total commitment to my craft; and Poseidon, the regent of the deep, as I spend half my life in water (small wonder I haven't developed webbed feet and gills). You are what you live by.

I like reading psychology books about what makes us work as humans and what gets in our way. Simon Sinek is the author of *Start with Why*. When 9/11 struck he was working for an advertising company close to the Twin Towers. The tragedy made him assess where he was going in life, and shortly after he left the company and set up his own enterprise. It was successful, and to the onlooker Sinek seemed as if he had nothing to complain about. However he still wasn't content; he felt a sense of disconnection and a lack of fulfilment in himself. He realised he had lost his passion and spark. He didn't know what his *why* was. Sinek has since made a fortune going into companies asking them *why* they do what they do rather than just what and how they do it. He discovered there was a pattern to those organisations who could answer clearly what their why was, such as Apple, whose aim was to challenge the status quo by thinking differently and making beautifully designed, simple, user-friendly computers.

If you apply this question to your own job and life and reflect that you're uninspired, it's probably because you've lost sight of – or have not yet discovered – your purpose. But don't worry, it's there just below the dust of everyday life, waiting to surface and dazzle.

Author Jon Gordon wrote: 'There is nothing more powerful than a humble person with a warrior spirit who is driven by a bigger purpose.' (source: Twitter) I love this quote, as my purpose these days is to inspire others to be better, as well as to be the best breaststroke swimmer there has ever been. At first it was just the desire for greatness powering my rocket, a need to quell the social inadequacy chip that sat like a monkey on my shoulder, glowering malevolently at the middle-class kids who had it easier than me growing up. They didn't sleep three to a room with their older brothers lighting up spliffs or crashing drunkenly through the door in the early hours, while they were trying to grab sufficient zeds to shine in their early professional sporting career. Growing up, I watched my brothers get into the wrong crowd and the problems that followed. Living in the same house with their addictive behaviour put a lot of pressure on all of us.

My purpose changed after Jim, my brother, briefly paused in his addiction to mamba and marijuana long enough to watch me win my first Olympic gold in Rio, and then having been inspired by it he began to address the demons in his mind and try to get clean. I was very proud of him and it made me so happy to see him kick mamba, a chemical cannabis, that turns you into a zombie. He's now a talented builder and a brilliant father and has left the drugs in the past (though he still likes a well-deserved pint after work!). Anyone who knows Jim will tell you what a professional, kind and warm-hearted person he is. The idea that I could help people through my swimming began to percolate in my mind and this has become my new purpose.

People seek different highs and I've got nothing against people taking drugs to numb and relieve the pain of their life. If it's a performance-enhancing drug you're taking, then on your bike, but I don't condemn recreational drugs, or natural highs. A lot of people around the world rely on alcohol, drugs and solvents to quieten the screaming in their head. That is their choice. I make no judgement. It's hard to communicate to the ones we love that all we want is what is best for them, and sometimes, that means keeping them at arms' length so they are forced to make positive change from within themselves.

Like Odysseus, the father of all travellers, we each have our life journeys to take and lessons to learn; sometimes we crash upon the rocks and sometimes we sail through unscathed and land on a beautiful island. It's our choice whether or not we learn from our falls.

I'm very grateful to have discovered my purpose so early. You may have to look for yours, or it might come as a calling at a moment when you don't expect it, when you feel at your least brave to explore it. But there will be no mistaking it when it arrives – it both lights you up inside and takes you outside your comfort zone.

A goal is an expression of your purpose. As you succeed in meeting the goals you set yourself, your purpose will change. Often, I say to the kids at my swim training clinics, 'You probably want to be the next generation of Olympians, but only a very few of you will succeed with that. But that's okay, because as we grow our purposes change. Many of you will eventually decide that instead of being a pro swimmer you want to be a doctor, a lawyer or a teacher or soldier. Purposes can be as temporary or as permanent as you want.'

When I started out my goal was to become the Olympic champion and it has now happened twice. For many years I focused on nothing else and slowly manifested it. Having achieved my goal, it no longer inspired me so I needed a fresh one to remotivate my sense of purpose. As soon as I finished in Rio, where I clocked 57.13 seconds, my goal then shifted to how I could take the winning margins even further. I worked really, really hard for the next three years for 0.2 seconds – which sounds insane! No normal person does that. Sometimes I look back at the journey to my first Olympics and think: 'I wish I had some of that raw, original purpose now.' As when you are young and hungry and climbing the ladder you have nothing to lose. On closer inspection of the time when I won my first Olympic gold, I had very few sponsors, wasn't earning much and the possibilities open to me were so much less than I have now. As humans we tend to look fondly back at the past rather than celebrating and being grateful for the *now*.

My purpose over the last three years has been shifting again as the next stage of my life after competitive swimming beckons on the not-too-distant horizon. I've recently become a father so I guess it's only natural that this has happened; I've shed the young single man's skin and am growing one of greater responsibility, and my interests are beginning to expand from swimming to admit new ventures.

Humans should always be adapting and moving on – I can't think of anything worse than being the same person every year. You want to be evolving, developing, your perspective always widening.

A person with a strong *why* is a dangerous force to be reckoned with

Friedrich Nietzsche, the German rebel thinker who det-onated an existential thought bomb in the dusty ranks of established nineteenth-century philosophy, said: 'The snake which cannot cast its skin has to die. As well, the minds which cannot change their opinions; they cease to be mind.' Nietzsche knew about struggle and adversity: he was constantly sick throughout his life, never had a loving relationship and spent much of his time alone before going insane and dying in a Basel asylum (tragically the same city where he had once shone so brightly as the university's youngest don). He's famous for that overused phrase: 'What doesn't kill you makes you stronger' – which is the basis for hard training and is core to this book – but the phrase that resonates most with me is, 'He who possesses a strong enough *why* can tolerate almost any *what*.' In other words, if you truly believe in doing something, you will walk across burning coals and through hell to serve that purpose; you'll be knocked down, but you will get up again and again even if your nose is bloodied.

You need a reason *why* you're prepared to put yourself through adversity and hardship to achieve your goal, otherwise your body and mind will rebel against that suffering. My goal to be the best swimmer in the world was powered by my why: to prove that a working-class kid who grew up without privilege could become world champion of what is a very middle-class sport. Nowadays, my why is to help people through my swimming, as well as to make something of my life and leave a legacy that will inspire young people to be their best selves, particularly my son George.

My race to the very top has been a long one, and 90 per cent of the time the battle has been between myself and the soldiers of self-doubt I have now learnt not to listen to. But that is all part of the journey of getting to know the real me. When I was seventeen, I was lucky enough to work with Bill Beswick, a brilliant sport psychologist responsible for enhancing the careers of the cream of British football, among many other stars from other sports. He taught me that the real battle is me versus me: my weak side against my strong side; my victim side against my fighter side. He also taught me not to fear the occasion but to embrace it as a warrior. I reckon all professional swimmers have to be a little mad, as most of their days they are following a black line underwater for hours on end.

I'm a firm believer that you get out what you put in, but first you need a reason for doing it. Remember Darren Hardy, our Irish endurance athlete with PTSD? He's a great example of the magic of a clear why. Recently, when he started losing toenails three marathons into a back-to-back five-marathon challenge and his resolve began to splinter, he reminded himself of the little girl with the rare degenerative brain condition for whom he was raising money and instantly found a second wind. Without his purpose of helping others welded to his need for a challenge it's doubtful that he would succeed in these extreme challenges he takes on.

Building a wall for money is not as satisfying as building a wall because you want to protect the people inside. It's the feeling it generates internally that brings meaning to why you are doing it. You're more likely to finish something if you are invested in it than if you're divorced from it. And you're even more likely to feel a stronger alignment with your purpose if it is something bigger than you, like running a marathon to pay for freshwater pumps in Malawi, or to raise funds for a little girl who is dangerously ill and needs a critical operation.

When I look back at the twelve years I've been working with my amazing coach and friend, Mel Marshall, I've had to endure some seriously gruelling corporal punishment to become world champion and accrue a haul of thirty-one international championship gold medals. Every year, in terms of training laps completed in the pool, I swim the equivalent of the Atlantic (at its narrowest point between Liberia and Brazil). When I first started working with Mel I was getting up at four o'clock every morning, going to the pool and training for two and a half hours before school, then back at school for six hours, then home to refuel for an hour before going to the pool again till ten at night. I was also training at the weekend.

My mum used to drive me the forty-minute journey to and from the pool on most mornings. Becoming a world-champion swimmer was a calculated risk I took very seriously, as it was a major investment of my youth and a huge sacrifice of sleep on my mum's part. I gambled all my chips on swimming, I put everything into my why and followed that river of ambition wherever it went. Was it a gamble? Looking back, I think it was the safest thing I could ever have done. My mindset was: 'Nothing is going to stop me getting a gold at the Olympics,' and gradually it began to happen. 'Besides,' I figured, 'If you're going to get up so early you may as well work like hell when you get there!' and I've never stopped since.

A goal without a plan is just a wish

To keep your motivation strong, you need to regularly check in with your goal to see if it still feeds your purpose. After the Rio Olympics, I needed something fresh to motivate me and push me through the pain of training. 'Project Immortal', created by Mel and myself, is our newest goal: to produce a performance so good it's almost inhuman and will *never* be beaten. I want to get to a place by the end of my career where people look at my personal best as something that cannot be beaten, that is so far ahead of the competition they won't even imagine breaking it. My current world record of 56.8 seconds for the 100m breaststroke is quick but it's not immortal ... yet!

Keeping note of where we are currently, where we want to get to, and planning how to get there is vital. In the sage words of Antoine de Saint-Exupéry: 'A goal without a plan is just a wish.' Keeping a journal is a great way to get familiar with patterns of behaviour you have that might be getting in your way. And making lists each day of what you need to do is an immediate test of whether you are being a Walter Mitty, just talking and dreaming, or you are taking action.

How to find your purpose

To find the truth within you you'll need to stop for long enough to listen to your inner voice. Ask it what makes you happy in life, what you would like to be remembered for and what is important to you. From your inner voice you will find clarity about what you want to strive for and what will fulfil you. Don't go looking for external things to give you your meaning – the answer lies within you. One way to access your truth is through meditation, being still and learning to listen to yourself. I take my quiet time very seriously as it is during these moments of peace that insights arise from within me.

*

I believe a lot of young people are lost in society at the moment because they haven't found the right purpose that gives them joy and a reason to believe in themselves. The effects of the Covid-19 pandemic on young people's mental health are only beginning to emerge, but certainly we know being kept away from the stimulation of learning, having O and A levels cancelled and losing access to friends and public sporting facilities – all of these things have had a hugely negative impact. Many are feeling rudderless, as if their lives lack any sense of meaning. Without purpose and a passion . . . 'Houston, we have a problem.'

The oldest and reportedly the happiest people on earth live on an island called Okinawa, off the coast of mainland Japan. Some of the natives attribute their longevity to the mild climate and their healthy diet of fresh fish and locally grown vegetables, and while these are both important contributors to good health (as they grow their own and fish themselves), there's more to it than that. *Ikigai* is the Japanese term for 'a reason to get up each morning' or 'that which gives you worth'. It's similar to what the French call '*raison d'être*', your reason for being.

Ikigai is about finding your joy in life through a sense of purpose, and scientists believe it can make you live longer. Blood tests on Okinawan pensioners revealed the presence of DHEA, a steroid hormone released by the adrenal glands that is produced when you are doing something you're interested in that gives you a sense of satisfaction. DHEA may well be the miracle 'longevity hormone' that scientists have been looking for, the holy grail that can stop ageing.

Okinawa is also home to more pensioners than anywhere else in Japan. As soon as they are able, young Okinawans head to the mainland to find work. The older members of the population have formed little cooperatives which grow vegetables and fruit, and fish together, as well as having a collective bank account with enough cash in it in the event of an emergency. These little pods of activity are socially binding and reassuring, and there's very little stress in Okinawans' lives. They also give the old people a sense of purpose: they are fishing and farming not just for themselves but others too. When I was in Tokyo for the 2021 Olympics, I witnessed this first hand; a lot of the older generation were provided with non-demanding jobs to keep them engaged and to feel valued.

Ikigai comes from the Japanese words *iki* meaning 'alive', and *gai* meaning 'worth'. We all need to locate and unlock our *ikigai* if we are to live fulfilling lives. What is your reason for being on this planet, what moves and inspires you? *Ikigai* is identified as a personal pursuit which is of benefit to others, and by doing it you experience an enhanced sense of meaning, purpose and self-fulfilment. We all have different reasons for getting up each morning, be it paying our mortgage, feeding our children or cat, or going to work; however, *ikigai* is not about drudgery or obligation, but the practice of doing something you are passionate about and good at, that pays you a wage you can happily live off and is of worth to society.

When you find your purpose something special happens – you wake up! It's as if you're emitting a new frequency because suddenly things in life begin to make more sense, to add up, and life and its opportunities come to – rather than run away – from you. People are drawn to an individual with a purpose that helps others and instinctively want to help them achieve their goals. As Muhammad Ali said: 'Service to others is the rent you pay for your room here on earth.' The things that excite you are clues to your passion which then will lead you to your why. In his book *The Third Way*, Dr Karl Phillips says: 'It is time for you to be a creator, an inventor, an experimenter, a risk taker, a rule breaker, a cultivator, a mistake learner, a fun seeker and a friend.' We can be so many things when we believe in ourselves.

Breaking down your goal

I break down my training year into a number of smaller cycles, for example September to December, January to April and April to July – that way I can periodise my training mode and my mindset. You can't go all guns blazing in September when you're training for an Olympic event the following July because it's not sustainable to work 110 per cent all the time – you'll burn out too quickly. Instead, you have to gradually build up to reach your peak of fitness and strength at the critical time.

I never start the season thinking I've got to get a 57.1 for the 100m breast, as it makes no sense thinking of the end. Instead, every day I micromanage my goals: for example, trying to lift the most weight I've ever lifted, or focusing on getting optimum efficiency on my turn. You don't get the end product without manufacturing it, and that might involve a thousand steps to get there. By focusing on the smaller details, the overall goal comes to you. I watched the 2012 Olympics and wished I could be half as great as that. I knew that to reach that standard I needed a better start, more strength and endurance, more power and a better technique. And that's exactly what we did. It wasn't just the stroke I needed to refine; I also had to develop from a boy to a man, as well as all the other stuff that wins an Olympic final: learning to deal with the pressure, to handle the crowd, the media, where your energy's going. You've got to break it all down, otherwise it's overwhelming.

Whether you're writing your first novel, running your first marathon or setting up a side hustle you need to map the territory first and do your homework. Remember *ikigai*: is your new calling going to give you a sense of meaning, is it something that makes you feel good and will be of service to others as well as you? Once you've selected your end goal you then do the homework for how to get there. What are the likely challenges, the time constraints, and are there any financial costs involved? Your strategy is your process, the route you'll follow to achieve your goal and fulfil your purpose. You need to figure out what the best strategy is, not the quickest, and from here create a timeline for your goal. If it's a one-year goal you need to break it down into single months, so the mountain is smaller.

Who can help you with your strategy? Do you know any experts who have been down the same road and might be able to mentor you? There's a saying, 'When the pupil is ready the teacher will appear.' In the UK we used to have a widespread tradition of apprenticeship where an aspiring craftsman – be it a carpenter, builder, plumber or electrician – would learn the ropes with a qualified elder who had the patience and the knowledge to pass on to them. These days young people are not keen to commit to a three-year stint. They're obsessed with instant gratification and validation. As a society we're addicted to the 'now culture' of getting everything as fast as possible to consume with minimum effort. If it's a mountain worth climbing, you'll do whatever is necessary to achieve your goal, and for however long it takes you to get there. And if you look hard enough, you'll find someone to help further your knowledge.

Don't be overwhelmed by your goal: start small and gradually increase the difficulty. If it's a 10-kilometre race you're building up to, start with 500 metres, build up to 1 kilometre and then 2 kilometres. Many people attempt to do too much in too little time and end up failing and abandoning their goal because they're frustrated. Make sure it's an attainable goal. And most importantly ensure that it is something you are clearly passionate about. If you are looking to climb Everest, you don't go straight for the peak. You have to have a strategy, moving gradually upwards from one camp to the next to acclimatise.

Step 2: Answer these four simple questions to find your *ikigai*

- What is my passion? (What inspires you?)
- What am I good at? (Consider your hobbies past and present, and things you have been curious about trying but haven't got around to.)
- What does the world need from me? (Can my purpose help others in some way?)
- What can I get paid for? (Is my passion something that I can monetise?)

Chapter Three

Finding Flow

My first international championship, the European Juniors, 2012.

I love the idea of the flow state, that place in yourself where you are in perfect sync with your body, mind and craft. My pre-flow state is the two-hour period before I race when I'm warming up, stretching off my muscles, rolling out my neck and spine, and summoning the right mindset. When I'm in the pool performing, I'm very much in the flow state because I'm fully prepared and I don't have to think about what I'm doing because it comes completely naturally – I'm in 'the zone'. According to Hungarian psychologist Mihaly Csikszentmihalyi, *flow* occurs when skills and the challenge at hand are equal. If they are not in equilibrium, for example if the challenge is too high for the skills, the person will become overawed and anxious; if too low they will become bored and distracted.

Mihaly (let's use his first name as none of us can pronounce Csikszentmihalyi!) coined the term 'flow state' in 1990, having grown up in wartime Europe during the Second World War and faced considerable adversity as a prisoner of war. After the war many had lost family members as well as their homes and jobs and were unable to find happiness and a sense of meaning. Having experienced pain and suffering on a wide scale Mihaly began investigating happiness. His studies drove him to believe that it was an internal state but one that could be generated with a committed effort. The psychologist interviewed athletes, musicians and artists to establish when they were at their most creative, productive and happiest. Many answered that they entered a place in themselves where their work sort of flowed out of them and they didn't have to try too hard, as in the doing of it they simply forgot about everything else – their focus on the task was absolute. We might call it 'being in the zone', or 'in your groove' or 'finding your mojo' . . .

The flow state is a crystallisation of experience and wisdom in your given pursuit meeting with fitness, preparation, confidence and passion to produce great results. It's when the muscle memory of all your training and prep meets a relaxed state in which you're able to be entirely in the moment like flowing water, your mind and body in concert making the right unconscious judgement calls and producing your best performance. I say 'unconscious', as flow is something which is believed to happen without the engagement of the prefrontal cortex of the brain, an area responsible for higher levels of cognitive function like self-reflective consciousness and memory. This is exactly what we don't want to be involved as this is where the inner critic lives – the one who tells you that you're ballsing it up, and that it's pointless carrying on painting that portrait because last time you got it wrong and you will again; or you're not good enough to beat the current champion (even though you've made it all the way through the tournament and you are currently playing against him) because your skills are not a match for theirs. Who do you think you are? it asks you.

Imagine you're walking along a two-foot wall; there is no consequence to falling off it as it is so low to the ground, so you don't worry about it, and besides, you tell yourself, 'It's easy, I have this covered.' Now I tell you that this wall is a hundred feet high and if you fall you will certainly die, just like the last person who attempted it did. Now your prefrontal cortex kicks in, alerting your critic who then reports it to your lizard brain, the old part of the brain. It then tells you you're in extreme danger and threatening your survival, quickly releasing cortisol, the stress hormone, to send you into flight mode so you get off the wall quickly.

Isn't it the same in so many areas of life when the stakes are suddenly much higher for someone and they talk themselves out of success and victory that is almost within their grasp? Like the actor who was brilliant in rehearsals and in his bathroom mirror, but who forgets his lines and stage directions when he's performing on press night; or the boxer who sparred brilliantly when relaxed in training but once in the ring, he allows his inner critic to take charge and he ends up 'choking', the opposite of being in the flow.

Don't try and fit in, be yourself

It's up to us how high we allow our mind to make that wall. At the European Juniors Championships in 2012, my lack of inner confidence disguised itself as being overly cocky. I thought, 'I'm going to conquer the world' but actually, I swam shit. In the 50m my trunks split down the crack of my arse and I didn't even get into the semis. Perhaps because I spent too much time looking at what the other swimmers were doing and exhausted myself trying to fit in socially with the team. Instead of worrying about winning I should have focused on my process. I even forgot why I'd started swimming in the first place, which was the enjoyment of travelling and my desire to race other people. I should have just flowed with that energy.

Trying to fit in is hard work, especially if you aren't being authentic to yourself. Sometimes it's hard enough being in our own skin, never mind trying to be another person we don't know. Know yourself and be comfortable and happy with who you are. Don't waste time on those who don't give you time back or try to diminish you. Remember, time and energy are so precious, perhaps the most valuable currencies there are. And never forget, the lion doesn't lose sleep over the opinions of sheep.

You've got to enjoy it to flow

Mihaly also asserted that to achieve flow the person must enjoy what they were doing for the sake of doing it (intrinsic motivation), rather than for reward (external motivation). As you head towards your peak fitness you are in a state of euphoric energy, which some call 'being in the flow' – an internal zone where you are at peace with yourself and your mind. In the flow state we are present, creative and intuitive, we trust our capability, our body responds well to us; we are not afraid of the unknown and are open to what it may bring. From the unknown we get insights and wisdom. And only by listening to it do we become who we really are. The ancient Greeks believed we should seek fulfilment rather than happiness, something they called *eudaimonia*: a process of satisfaction found in successfully persevering through difficult challenges. It's here that we learn what we are really made of.

The opposite of flow is when our mind goes back to its default setting, known as 'the computer state' referred to earlier, whereby it cross-references similar situations we have experienced to inform its response to new situations. Often these are way off target, as the brain, being subject to around 100,000 thoughts per day, does its best to approximate and take shortcuts to save time. As a result, we can very easily sleepwalk through life relying on our inner computer. Every champion always has moments of doubt somewhere along their journey. It's choosing to use that doubt as fuel for your purpose; using that borderline feeling of fight or flight that it brings to propel you forward.

When you are in flow, nothing that is thrown at you will divert you from your path. Some would call it a war path, a clear route to follow that helps you achieve your goal in the long run. Make small adjustments – like having a timer on your phone to protect you from disappearing down a rabbit hole on Twitter, Facebook, Instagram or whatever it might be and wasting hours on them. Distractions will take you off your war path if you're not careful. The clearer your end point, your goal, the straighter your road to get there.

Researchers have long sought the ingredients for getting into this state, and a 2015 study featured in ScienceAlert (sciencealert.com) conducted by Swann and Scott Goddard at the Southern Cross University in Australia, reveals a second flow state known as 'the clutch state'.

The clutch state

In the study, sixteen professional athletes were interviewed directly after competition while their memories were still fresh. The results showed there was a slightly different second state which appeared within the flow state. The athletes reported a sense of control over their performance, a slowing down of time, a heightened level of confidence and an enhanced motivation to succeed. It sounds fairly similar to how you might describe the flow state, but a few things were markedly different: the athletes were highly *aware* of their thoughts and feelings during the competition, their skills were working automatically, and they were completely focused.

The essential difference between flow and clutch is that flow is about relaxing and letting it happen, while clutch is about *consciously* trying to make it happen. The clutch state is when the athlete thrives under pressure (the polar opposite of choking) and is able to consciously up their game and be their best at critical junctures of a performance. There is no fear, no self-censoring; the athlete is completely aware of themselves and decides it is the critical time to change gear. Take Muhammad Ali versus George Foreman in the classic Rumble in the Jungle fight in Zaire in 1974. After taking a bit of a hiding in the first couple of rounds from the current champion, Ali realised he wasn't strong enough to fight him toe to toe, so he switched to 'rope-a-dope', tiring Foreman out by taking punches from the other man as he covered up and leant back on the ropes. Each time he was hit the damage of the blow would travel through his body and into the ropes rather than stop at his body. Ali was hyper-alert, dodging blows – it seemed as if he was able to slow time right down for his shaping. Having tired out the slugging Minotaur, Ali felled him in the eighth round.

When we are in flow, what we feel, what we wish and what we think are in harmony. It occurs when a person faces a clear set of goals that require appropriate responses. Flow activities provide immediate feedback and make it easy to gauge how well you are doing. For flow to work, a person's skills must be fully involved in overcoming a challenge that is just about manageable for them. When flow is in motion time distorts and hours seem to pass in minutes.

When you watch me swim, I certainly don't look happy. I'm concentrated grimly on the task at hand: to finish first and dominate. Only after the task is completed do I look back on what has happened, fully appreciate it and bask in the achievement. You can only experience rare epiphanies like seeing whales and dolphins next to you by pushing yourself out of your comfort zone. Ross Edgley says he's always been chasing sunrises and sunsets.

Csikszentmihalyi believed: 'The quality of life, what we do and how we feel about it will be determined by our thoughts and emotions. When we feel active and strong we are also more likely to feel happy. Most people feel they're more cheerful and sociable when they're with others than when they're alone.' Curiously, the Greek word 'idiot' originally meant someone who lived by themselves, cut off from community interaction. Being with friends provides the most positive experiences.

How can you return to the flow state? By learning new skills and increasing your challenges.

Step 3: Banishing negativity

To train yourself to be more conscious of negative thoughts and halt them in their tracks, wear a simple elastic rubber band on your wrist. Each time you hear your inner critic or a negative unhelpful thought, pull the band and give yourself a sharp twang, then replace the negative with a positive thought (or statement of gratitude). Very soon you'll begin to change the quality of your thinking because your brain will associate negative thinking with pain.

Chapter Four

Welcoming Pain

Extremely exhausted on my AP race tour, 2021.

Rumi, the famous Persian poet, once said, 'The cure for the pain is in the pain.' He was talking about emotional self-learning rather than suffering endless laps in a swimming pool, but the same can be said for the benign pain created by extreme exercise. The body's ability to seek and maintain a stable internal state, whereby your immune system is working, your temperature is level and heart pumping effectively is called homeostasis. To improve your fitness levels you must expose your body to stress and disrupt this homeostasis – that's to say, put the body through some pain. There is no fitness fairy tale; you're going to have to suffer and gasp for breath, feel your lungs on fire, muscles seizing up, the burn in your arms . . . if you're to improve. Adaptation is the term applied to the body's physiological response to training, and how it copes with the new load.

Ross Edgley, who spent five months in the sea swimming around Britain, concluded that the human body is not supposed to marinate in salt water for weeks on end. He suffered 'salt tongue', where bits of his tongue started falling out of his mouth into his food, but he continued nonetheless. After two weeks, he was so exhausted he had to stop looking at how far he had left to go on the tracker and focus instead on one stroke at a time. Skin was falling off him in his wetsuit, with open wounds across his body. He suffered sleep deprivation, hallucinations. But it's hard to beat a man who doesn't quit. It took Ross a hundred and fifty-seven days (five months), swimming six hours on six hours off, to swim 1,780 miles round Britain. The biggest battle was in his head, not with his body. 'I knew my body could take it.'

While Ross was swimming the Scottish phase of his Herculean swim, his dad was diagnosed with terminal cancer. Ross wanted to quit the swim, but his dad insisted he finish what he had started and keep going. His dad was his common sense, his compass, and his dying wish became like a band of steel strengthening his son's purpose. I get that completely now that I'm a father; I have someone else to swim for that spurs me on and makes all the pain worthwhile.

Why are some people more resistant to pain than others? We all have the potential to develop a higher tolerance for pain, and nor is it about creating a masochistic mindset either. I wasn't born with a higher pain tolerance, it's something that I've built up over time by immersing myself in discomfort. Your tolerance to pain naturally increases as you get used to it. According to *Forbes* magazine: 'Pain is not just a mindset, it's a journey. Your tolerance for pain rises and falls depending on what's happening in the rest of your life.'

There have been many times in my career that Mel has

set me an epic challenge that I thought I couldn't complete, at least until I got my claws into it. Many years ago, there was a major turning point in my approach to training. One dreary Monday dawn somewhere in Derby, she said I couldn't go home until I had completed the task to a certain level, nor did I want to go home until I'd demolished it. I welcomed the pain and suffering and the whingeing voice inside my head telling me 'This is too much, you're tired . . . just go home to your warm comfortable house.' I knew that champions are no strangers to discomfort, that this is what moulds them, and that I had to keep going through my pain barrier. Since that day I have never wavered or stopped, it was a day when the bar was raised. It is my sheer determination to never give up that has separated me from the average swimmer.

The Iceman

Dutchman Wim Hof is also known as The Iceman. His exploits in freezing temperatures certainly warrant the moniker: he's climbed Everest in shorts, been placed in a giant jar of ice for almost two hours where he demonstrated that he could control his body's core temperature, as well as running a half-marathon in the snow. Hof is famous for the technique he has developed using a combination of cold-water immersion, controlled breathing and mental focus to achieve what would appear to be the impossible.

Cold-water immersion places the body in physical stress, and by learning to process the pain we are able to deal with its discomfort. Hof has taught himself to control his autonomic nervous system, which means he can increase his adrenaline levels at will. Humans are not supposed to be able to do this; it's – and there's that word again – impossible. Hof treats his body as a laboratory and has demonstrated his ability to activate his immune system. We'll revisit one of his introductory exercises at the end of this chapter.

Nietzsche said of pain: 'I assess the power of a will by how much resistance, pain and torture it endures and knows how to turn to its advantage.'

I am addicted to going into my workplace every day, hammering it and coming out tired and smiling. I don't see the point in giving just 80 or 90 per cent. I love pushing myself to new limits in search of finding the edge on the next person. It sounds strange but the more pain I go through, the better I feel.

There are three different kinds of pain: pain from injury, pain from threat and euphoric pain, which comes as a reward from extreme effort and doesn't harm us. It's the latter that I like! We have different nerves in our body, some with sensory receptors that respond to heat and burning cold, others to pressure. We also have non-specific, high-threshold nerves that it takes a lot to activate. This information is sent to the brain which asks itself if it is something we have experienced before: is it a burn, a cut, a break? . . . It then decides whether to tell us we are in pain and the appropriate level to administer.

This output is like a fire alarm; while the sound is always the same it can be triggered by different things: a house fire, smoke from burnt toast, or the alarm's battery getting low. When we experience pain it is real but not necessarily *valid*; sometimes it's just the survival mechanism in the brain being hysterical. Our bodies will do their best to protect us even when it's not absolutely necessary, and it's possible to work through certain kinds of pain without causing damage to ourselves. The great myth is that pain *always* equals injury, that if something hurts it must have been as a result of doing something damaging.

The medical definition of pain is 'an unpleasant sensory and emotional experience, which is related to or described in terms of actual or potential tissue damage.' So, pain is also about *threat*. It's a known fact that when we are placed under extreme stress, be it impending danger or during attack, among the many chemicals in the body that are emitted to save us is analgesia, which enables a person to ignore excruciating pain until they are out of harm's way. It's also experienced by athletes locked in the furnace of competition, like former WBO super-middleweight champion Joe Calzaghe who broke his left hand in the first few rounds against the Kenyan, Evans Ashira, but fuelled by his force of will, adrenaline and analgesia, he boxed his way to a points victory with just his right arm.

In his book *Break Point*, ex-special forces soldier and

mindset guru Ollie Ollerton recounts how having been disqualified on his first attempt to pass 'Selection', the gruelling six-month assessment process for the world's toughest military elite, the SAS and SBS, he was on his second attempt the following year. A gifted cross-country runner, all was going well until he sprained his ankle and could no longer walk. The military doctor informed him he'd actually broken it. Ollerton knew he wouldn't be allowed another attempt at Selection (maddeningly, he was very close to the end of the six months' assessment). He doggedly rejected the advice of the doctor and refused to be pulled out, strapping his ankle up with so much tape he could barely move his foot. Somehow, his determination outweighed his pain and he prevailed through the final days of Selection hell.

As we know, 'adaptation' is the idea that you have to disrupt your body's natural equilibrium to improve and stretch its performance. Special forces training requires soldiers to be pushed beyond their perceived limits of endurance, as it's only by visiting these hidden reservoirs and learning to smash through the usual walls of fatigue and fear that they can adapt. David Goggins believes: 'We have 80% more capacity for endurance than we are tapping into. Because in this other 80% is suffering, pain, failure, self-doubt, darkness and a whole bunch of light. But to get to the light we have to go through a world of shit.'

At twenty-four, Goggins was a massively overweight 300 pounds. One night he saw a documentary about 'Hell Week', the torturous water-based trials would-be recruits for the

Navy Seals have to undergo to be accepted into this hallowed military elite. Goggins decided he had a choice: either carry on being the broken figure he was or change his life. To get in the frame for Hell Week he needed to drop 106 pounds in less than three months. He had to 'invent a person who could take any pain, any suffering . . . had to build this calloused mind through suffering.' Through obsessive exercise, come rain or shine, and the sole purpose to make the Navy Seals, he lost the weight and got in.

The question you might be asking is: 'How do I access this 80 per cent reserve of energy?' I wish I could say otherwise but every record I've ever broken was founded on the pain I went through to achieve that speed. If you want your mind and body to adapt their pain tolerance there is no other way but to face pain head-on and cut through it like an airborne *Peaky Blinders* cap! As Joe Rogan says: 'We've been fed this horse-shit line that we're supposed to seek comfort. I don't think you are. I think we're supposed to seek lessons and seek difficult tasks and accomplishments that are hard to do.'

The pleasure of pain

Endorphins are neurotransmitters which stimulate neurons to reduce pain, and are produced by the brain when we're injured, having sex or doing strenuous exercise. If we push ourselves hard enough in training, endorphins can in turn activate the release of dopamine, which produces feelings of euphoria. We've all heard the term, 'No pain, no gain.' Where extreme exercise is concerned (as opposed to injury), pleasure is indeed the gain that comes from pain. Endorphins stimulate the brain's release of serotonin and melatonin which transforms painful experiences into pleasure. The high you experience from punishing yourself corresponds to how hard you push yourself. The greater the effort, the bigger the high.

I remember there was this time when I was training at Repton school for the 2016 Olympics. The school had great gym facilities, good management and people who under-stood exactly what I needed in my prep. No offence to Derby Council but this was a place that you could get shit done without getting mired in red tape. It was the 2nd of January, dark and hopeless, with that post-Christmas and New Year blues we often feel, where everything feels like an effort.

I needed a challenge, something that would give me a sense of achievement and a rush of endorphins. I told Mel this and she was straight on it, almost as if she knew what I had been thinking. The set was a 500 maximum row, then into a hundred reps of a chosen exercise – be it bench press, dips, chin-ups or squats – 10 times. I couldn't move a single limb afterwards, every muscle in my body ached, but the rush of endorphins popping through me made all the pain worthwhile. What had been a grey and formless day was now vivid with possibility.

It's not just dopamine and endorphins, serotonin and

melatonin that the brain produces to numb and reward the pain caused by intense exercise; adrenaline is also produced, raising the athlete's heart rate and capability. Curiously, seeking pain is a uniquely human pursuit. When we perform any sport requiring extreme physical exertion, potential damage caused by overactivity is automatically prevented by the arrival of lactic acid, which makes our muscles burn and forces us to stop. But it's how we choose to process this pain that counts.

Let's look at an example of the body playing cautious caretaker. Freediving is one of the most dangerous sports you can undertake and involves dropping down to sunless depths in the ocean on a single breath of air. It's not just about the journey down, the freediver must allow themselves to get back up to the surface again. According to ABC News, the sport claims around a hundred lives per year.

Freedivers divide their dive into four stages:

1. the Awareness Phase – the mind tells you it is time to surface and breathe
2. involuntary contractions in your diaphragm, the result of carbon dioxide build-up
3. a rush of fresh oxygenated blood from the spleen allowing you to carry on a bit further
4. the larynx closes reflexively to keep water out of your lungs, placing your body on stand-by, then you black out.

The trick freedivers learn is to make sure they're well within the first three stages and never stray to stage four. Our body will try and save us but once we have passed its warning signs it's down to us how far we push ourselves.

If freedivers can access this hidden reserve of oxygen and we really do have untouched fuel in the reserve tank, why don't more of us experience it? We've all heard stories about people in extreme situations doing extraordinary things by accessing hidden strength. Only today on Twitter I saw an old man wade into a pond to rescue his spaniel which had been taken by an alligator – he grabbed it, forced its jaws open and freed his dog. What makes us take these risks? When danger, in whatever form it appears, threatens a loved one, that is usually sufficient to bring out our inner caveman and our desire to fight.

In 1989 an American called Tom Boyle demonstrated this hidden reserve when he saw the car ahead knock down a cyclist and drag him under its fender. Boyle ran to the aid of the cyclist, lifting the Camaro's front wheels clean off the ground so he could escape. Boyle was no wimp – he'd dead-lifted 700 pounds before, but the car weighed 3,000 pounds. For a brief period, he was possessed by a strength unknown to him. It was only after the drama died down that Boyle realised he had been gritting his teeth so hard while lifting the car that he had shattered eight of his teeth.

Welcoming pain and how I work through it

I have always used the aggressive part of me in a very positive way to go through the pain; the more pain I went through, the more mad it made me. It was almost like I went out of my way to find the pain as I knew it would make me successful. I never turn up at the pool and say to myself: 'Today I've got 20 × 100m to swim and it's going to be hard work and I don't have much energy.' Instead, I always look at it like, 'If I swim it hard, today's session will make me fitter, more powerful and a better athlete.' I see pain as an opportunity not a hindrance. Also, I think about what my opponents will be doing and how hard they must be working, and like rocket fuel that propels me forward to work even harder.

I always believe that your body can go further, that there is more fuel in your tank and you've just got to be able to push forward to tap into it. What is your limit? A mile or five miles? The more you do the further that limit stretches, and the only real limit is that which you put inside your head. It's about having the right attitude to performance from the start. So, for example, if I was going to do a crazy, crazy hard set my attitude at the start would always be, 'Right, let's conquer this, let's get to the middle.' And when I get to the middle I say, 'Okay, not far to go now.' I break each set down into achievable pieces, break it down so it's not this overwhelming, titanic task ahead of me.

Obviously through training you're going to slow down or

get niggles that may stop you, but it's the consistency with which you do things that counts. You're going to have that desire to slow down – it's natural to want to be able to stop and be comfortable – but no one's ever got anywhere great through being comfortable. And for me that's the method to the madness. I like being outside my comfort zone because it's where growth happens and it helps me become a faster, better, more resilient athlete, both mentally and physically.

The more you turn up the more you get used to the pain. I don't think it was ever a light-bulb moment, but if I'd had a bad competition, for example, or didn't get the results I wanted, it always sent me into a frenzy to train harder, be more accurate and just be more resilient. So, I guess the more of a loss I took and the harder the fall, the better the rebound. The only way you can find out what you're really made of is by pushing yourself to those untravelled places.

Step 4: Cold shower every morning

Take a cold shower each morning. Breathe though your nose deeply, exhaling shallowly and quickly from your mouth. Try and breathe in thirty times and, on the thirtieth exhalation, count how long you can last without taking another breath. You'll be very surprised. This is a brilliant way of putting your body under stress in a controlled environment, so when the real thing comes along your body is more comfortable dealing with it.

Chapter Five

Cultivating Positivity – Getting in the Right State to Perform

At MediaCity in Salford after the 2015 World Championships in Kazan, Russia.

Cultivating Positivity – Getting In the Right State to Perform

I wanted to be a jet fighter pilot, but Fate took me to the pool instead (besides, at 6 feet 3 inches I'm much too tall to fit into a cockpit!). You play the cards life gives you. I discovered that breaststroke was my forte and, around 2014, I began to put everything into maximising that talent. A gladiator mindset is one in which we blame no one for our lack of success, take responsibility for our actions, stop avoiding things we're scared of, or bitching about what we haven't got, and take charge of our destiny. We fight our way through or around whatever the block is before us and refuse to be diminished by our doubts and demons. We never give up. Gladiators have a very clear view of the light at the end of the tunnel and where we want to get to, and whatever Minotaur or harpies we need to contend with en route, nothing will stop us. Self-belief is our ammunition.

We have tremendous ability in all of us to effect meaningful change in our lives, but this will only happen if we get into a positive mindset. We live in an age which is rife with anxiety, and personally I blame social media, a lack of work–life balance and an enduring obsession with possessing shiny stuff we think will make us happy – of which I'm guilty. There's nothing wrong with wanting nice things for you and your family, but a life of substance is not reliant on possessions, it's about who you are inside and the way you treat others. I know I've made mistakes and have put people at the back of my thoughts when they should have been at the forefront. But you can't change the past, only learn from it.

Most of us are unfulfilled because we live our lives from the 'outside in' rather than the 'inside out' – that's to say our happiness is based on other people's opinions of us, and we obsess about the things that we haven't got rather than being thankful for what we have. Living from the inside out is taking the time to slow down, shutting out external influences like social media, and getting to know your real inner self. It's from here that we find truthful meaning and real wealth. If you find yourself addicted to the way the world views you, I suggest you put down your phone for a few days, leave it at home and take yourself into nature. Go right into the wilderness and take a map – not a virtual one! – and feel your anxieties start to wash away.

The good news is once you've become more cognisant of the way you are mentally wired you can start to be a little more conscious of what you're letting into your head. It's not long before you start to see real positive change.

How easy is it to slip into negativity?

Would you let a burglar into your house? I assume the answer is no but if you can view negative thoughts as intrusive burglars of the mind looking to rob your positivity, it is easier to lock them out. And yet we allow negative thoughts to roam freely around our mind like school bullies. The Stoics talked of the need for us to 'keep watch over the enemy of yourself'. The enemy is our automatic side, the lazy response system and tendency towards sloth and taking the easy route. It's the side of us that automatically takes no responsibility for our actions, that blames things on everyone else, that considers itself the victim. The mind is like an open gate to a field, you have to keep watch over it constantly because if you walk away from the gate for just a moment, negativity will slip through. I doubt myself as does everyone at times, but I work through these doubts, examining the veracity of the thoughts that gave rise to them, and then I delete the offenders.

How conscious are you in your everyday life? Do you drive to a place only to arrive and wonder how you got there? Do the weeks seem to drift into each other with little to distinguish them? Are you putting days in your life or life in your days? There is a massive difference between the two. Before we know it, time has passed through our hands like a fistful of sand and it's game over. But it doesn't have to be like this; we can choose to climb off that conveyor belt bound for the land of mediocrity at any time, so long as we have the desire within us to effect change and are prepared to make sacrifices, learning to be comfortable in uncomfortable places.

Our lives are not just a long continuum of time. Nobody is saying that we must do the same thing as we did the week before; we can stop, pause and take a look at where we want to go and change direction *whenever* we want. We are our own captains plotting our own route.

Taking control of the control centre

The first thing we must do before anything else is realise that success starts in the mind, and until we take charge of that control centre by monitoring negative thoughts and focus on feeding ourselves with positive messages and affirmations, we will struggle to get anywhere. What you put into your mind dictates what happens next in your life. If you bought a supercar would you run it on the cheapest fuel and oil, or to get the best out of its engine would you be more mindful of the quality of what you were putting into it? Thoughts are no different; if you want your mind and body to run smoothly you need to be as vigilant as a watchdog.

How thoughts work

The lens through which we see the world is built upon the beliefs we've established over many years based on our experiences, as well as the opinions of others which have been impressed on us. That doesn't necessarily make either of them correct, as often these beliefs are outdated and need reviewing. Beliefs give rise to thoughts which create feelings that cause us to act. Depending on whether those thoughts are actively positive ones intentionally fed by us, or unconsciously negative, we will end up with a given result. If we leave the thought unchecked it might be an old negative belief making us feel and act in a correspondingly negative way which is reflected in what we get in life. Given that our nature is one that veers between overcautious and anxious, if we don't actively cultivate a bold mindset nothing positive can happen. A Spartan never went into battle thinking he would lose; it wasn't even a question in his mind. Just as a gladiator didn't allow himself to think it would be his last visit to the coliseum as he stood in the dark tunnel waiting for the hatch to open.

So long as you are not dying or in imminent danger, your mind views this as adequate. But were you born to accept adequate? You may be in an unsatisfactory relationship with someone who diminishes you, or in a job that is killing your soul, or maybe living in a cold-water flat with mould on the walls; if you're still alive and not actively threatened your brain will discourage you from seeking out a better alternative. The bottom line is we tolerate being in unsatisfactory situations because we're scared of change. When we start understanding that the brain is just trying to keep us safe and then continue to push through it, we begin to move from where we are stuck to where we *want* to be.

To be the best athlete in the world I have to be at the front of the ship. There is no point doing something if you don't understand why you are doing it, or have the desire to do it, as you won't be one hundred and ten percent committed to it. We must know where we want to be deep down, and if the goal seems too great to achieve then that's the best feeling as you have an amazing challenge ahead of you!

Be your own best coach

There's a great old Roman saying, '*Vincit qui se vincit*', meaning: 'He conquers who conquers himself.' In other words, if you can learn to see through, question and silence your inner critic and fear of change you can begin to learn to listen to the deeper you from within. Stop trying to impress others and impress yourself instead; self-esteem is not an egoistic state, it's one in which you respect yourself and do yourself justice. The journey to greatness begins with your opinion of yourself, so you need to learn to encourage your spirit when you're down or feel like you've lost your way. Be your own coach and psychologist, start to become your own best observer. Whatever your history may be, whatever your current situation, your future is unwritten – within reason (and sometimes without it) you *can* do and become anything. Trust yourself to go through the tunnel of perceived pain to necessary change and you'll find it's not as bad as your kneejerk survival instinct tells you it is. Steve Jobs once said: 'Have the courage to follow your heart and intuition. They somehow know what you truly want to become.'

Nobody knows you better than you!

When we find genuine silence in our mind, even for a second or two, rather than being informed by outside influences, our inner voice speaks profound truths to us, and if we are open to its wisdom it will begin to give us more and more deeper insights into ourselves. If this sounds like I've just climbed out of a Californian oxygen capsule and I'm babbling New Age bollocks, bear with me.

It's easy to tell the difference between your inner self and your inner critic: one makes you feel strong, the other reduces you with self-doubt. Buddhists meditate in search of a few moments of fleeting mental peace. If you can find time to practise a simple breathing-led meditation at the beginning of each day which allows you to consciously inhabit your body and feel present in your mind, it will put you in a good place to take charge of your day.

Peak achievers discipline their minds to support them. By programming powerful thoughts of what we want and repeatedly visualising achieving our goal clearly in our mind we can begin to change the lens we look through. You get what you think, and if you keep picturing the best outcomes the mind shifts to being more automatically positive. The brain is hard at work satisfying your primary needs of finding food, procreating and sleeping, as well as regulating breathing, pumping your heart and maintaining your temperature, and constantly monitoring the environment around it. In fact, the brain is so tied up with these vital tasks it cuts corners; in any new situation you find yourself in it will fire off an email to your memory bank to dig up the old data from previous similar experiences and the way we responded to them, picking a response which is the closest match. Very often it's a lazy response and isn't the right one, or if the memory bank has nothing similar to offer, the brain will send you fear to stop you doing something new. What you think is the real world around you is simply a perspective concocted through the filter of past experience. In his book *You Are the Placebo: Making Your Mind Matter*, Joe Dispenza alleges that the majority of our thoughts each day are no different to the day before, as we are on autopilot. Our brains from the moment we wake are looking for problems that may threaten our existence and tend towards the negative. Every memory we have of a place or person has corresponding thoughts and feelings attached to it, so given that our responses are mostly automatic shortcuts it means we are constantly living old, negative emotions. New conscious thoughts lead to new positive behaviours.

Next time you feel depressed, demotivated or disillusioned, notice what your thinking has been over the last couple of minutes. If it's creating something negative, redirect it to the opposite. For example, when that inner critic (which we all have) is spouting its usual crap: 'Nothing ever changes, I am going to be in the same dead-end job this time next year,' try flipping it to: 'Everything is changing for the better and this time next year I know I will be in the job I love.'

Whatever we are feeling we will attract more of it: worry attracts worry, dissatisfaction creates dissatisfaction, and before you know it you're in a downward spiral. We need to consciously send positive messages to not only ourselves but the universe too. This quote from *The Secret Daily Teachings* by Rhonda Byrne sums it up nicely: 'Your life is a reflection of what you hold inside you, and what you hold inside you is always under your control.'

Visualisation

I visualise specifically what I want out of my life as if it is in the cross hairs of a sniper's rifle. I'm continually asking myself, 'If I did this or won that what would my life be like as a result?' Whatever the outcome you want, focus intently on it, keep thinking about it, visualise it so your mind has a clear idea of where it must go. Taste the moment and how you will feel, how it will improve the lives of others, and then watch it appear. Then keep doing it.

New habits take very little time to establish and the more we live our values and behave in a positive manner, the more it conditions the mind and body to follow. Some say you can completely turn your way of thinking around in as little as a month. The average life is around a thousand months in total, so one month's hard focus and vigilance seems a very small price to pay.

Six things that get in our way

Shaolin monks who dedicate their lives to letting go of the dissatisfaction caused by unchecked thoughts identify six common hindrances that get in our way:

- essential desire – being obsessed with external material things
- negative frequency – giving off negative vibrations instead of positive ones
- sloth and laziness – allowing our fear of change to turn into apathy
- lack of purpose – without a 'why' we're lacking meaning
- restlessness and unsettled mind – 100,000 thoughts per day
- self-doubt – our inner critic will reinforce its low opinion of us with evidence of past failures and examples of our worst self.

Just because you think it, doesn't mean it's real

Worrying about 'what ifs' – things that haven't happened yet – is a waste of energy. Humans are either agonising about the future or are stuck in something that happened in the past, an old script that needs discarding. To bring harmony to our lives we need to master ourselves first. Our problem is that we are hard-wired for comfort while the essence of our soul seeks fresh growth. And we scare too easily. Just because your thinking tells your body to make you anxious and fearful about something, it doesn't mean it is real. While there are genuinely scary and life-threatening episodes in our lives which merit genuine fear, many of our day-to-day worries are based on worst-case *what-if* scenarios which we indulge and blow out of proportion.

Remember when you were a teenager and you got back late because you missed a bus or walked a friend back, and when you finally returned home, your phone empty of battery, you were met by a near-tearful or hysterical parent whose imagination had spiralled out of control as they had catastrophised all the bad things that might have happened to you? Left alone with our thoughts this is what happens if we don't take control. When we experience that sense of dread in our stomachs, we need to be really present and ask ourselves in the moment, 'What is my thinking doing and is it serving my purpose?' The easiest way to earth your hysterical inner voice is to question it. Is it F.E.A.R. – False Expectation that Appears Real – or is it a genuine threat?

Failure to practise this self-mastery results in living our lives on constant low alert, the body overproducing cortisol.

A thought process that has helped me considerably through this is becoming a master of living in the present. Stop worrying about things in the future that may never happen, stop bathing in the mistakes and victories you made in the past. All that you can change is the present, the right now. The present defines your future and every thought feeling and action informs what will happen next. Why delay till tomorrow what you can start today?

It's interesting that in some parts of the world we are contributing less to our pensions than ever, preferring to enjoy the 'now' instead. I was guilty of this too, wondering what the point of saving all that cash was when I might get run over tomorrow? We are forgetting to visualise our older self, the one who will be weaker and more reliant than we are now. We all want to be comfortable in retirement so it's a vital conversation we need to be having with ourselves.

Flush away unhelpful thinking

One habit I've developed that has really helped me over the last five years when my thinking is in a negative place, when I feel depressed or am self-doubting, is to open a conversation with that dominant negative thought. If, for example, it's telling me: 'You're not good enough on the back end of a 50m,' I examine that statement and ask myself: 'Why do you think you are struggling on the back end of a 50m?' Then I might answer: 'Well it wasn't much good because I'm tired and I've been training really hard, or perhaps it's because . . .' Just by having a dialogue and finding an explanation for the negative feeling and thought, you are able to nullify and disempower it, then flush it away. It's about learning to have an honest conversation with yourself, and it's helped me to be happier in my own skin.

I work hard, but so does that undermining voice in my head that is *so* quick to criticise me. Getting older is about learning to like yourself and not giving yourself such a roasting. So these days I treat myself with respect and my thoughts with scepticism if they are pulling me down, constantly examining if they are legitimate or not. In 2019, I got to the point where I was tired of having negative thoughts. Like individual fish they'd quickly spawn into shoals of self-criticism. I asked myself why I was feeling like that and resolved to approach everything with a more positive attitude, to have a better energy and be dedicated to giving myself affirmative messages. I have practised positive self-maintenance ever since.

Becoming your own superman

In 1883 Friedrich Nietzsche wrote *Thus Spoke Zarathustra*, in which he describes the 'superman' (or higher man) and his will to self-power. He encourages us to be our own critic and coach with our own moral code and natural compass guiding us towards what is true and just, without being told what to do by society. We can only fulfil our potential by not being a sleepwalking herd creature, he says, by trusting in our own actions and believing in ourselves, driven by the fuel of our own willpower. To become like the higher man, we have to be people of action, walk our talk, and not fear standing up as individuals for what we believe in; we should have the courage to go our own way and shine a light which is so bright it can't be ignored. The higher man sees through their plan by adopting a non-self-critical mindset that allows them to see their failures as par for the course.

Instead of just accepting what we are told we have to think and ask our own questions without fear of being rejected by the group (society, the herd) or ridiculed for being different. The establishment fears pioneers of new ideas – like Jesus, Buddha and Martin Luther King – because they threaten the status quo and what the naysayers blindly believe in since they are too scared of being individuals themselves. To maximise your potential, you *have* to take the path less trodden. To be free you must be independent and self-knowing. Personally, I have always preferred to stand apart from the herd. Sometimes I didn't have the courage to back myself and other times it misfired, but I kept pushing myself and exploring my limits. I knew there was more to life than just following everyone else down the same path. Robert Frost once wrote: 'Two roads converged in a wood, and I took the one less travelled by, and that has made all the difference.'

For Nietzsche it was vital we understood what motivated us to make important decisions in our life. We are unique, each and every one of us, and we have to find our uniqueness. We need to be open and say *yes* to the things in our life that give us meaning. *'Amor fati'* is a Stoic phrase which translates as 'love your fate' – the good, bad and ugly, all of the things you've succeeded or failed at have brought you on the path to where you are right now. You are where you are supposed to be at this very moment.

Whoever told you that you can't do something, be it a teacher or friend or relative, is probably threatened by your potential for success and envious of your fearlessness. There's a story my coach Mel sometimes tells which reminds me of this: 'In 2013 at the British coaches' conference, after Adam had achieved 59 seconds for the 100m breaststroke as an eighteen-year-old, I said, "This kid is going to swim 57 seconds one day." There was a ripple of laughter. But I knew he would do it and he went on to prove me right.'

As Marianne Williamson said, 'Our deepest fear is not that we are inadequate. Our deepest fear is that we are powerful beyond measure. It is our light, not our darkness, that most frightens us.'

Take a risk before you die

My interests are quite eclectic, and I was watching something on YouTube the other night about space and how limitless the universe is. Apparently there are more stars in our universe than there are grains of sand on every beach in the world if you added them all up. But the distance between each star is so vast that it would take Voyager 2 – our current furthest operating spaceship – 80,000 years to get to the next star. The visuals zoomed out from Earth to Mars, then the rest of the outer planets and beyond, eventually to the Milky Way, but it didn't end there, zooming out through our cosmic group of galaxies then on to *other* universes . . . It made me realise how small and insignificant we are and how little time we are here for. When we look at time and space abstractedly like that we may as well put all our gambling chips on one number and go for it. What is the worst thing that can happen? At least we tried.

We all die. No matter how much money you have, you can't cheat death; however if you can create memorable change, you become immortal. I think of the legacy left behind by people like Muhammad Ali and Martin Luther King. I want to inspire others after I'm gone and while I'm here. Death is not something that waits patiently in the distant shadows of old age, it's with us every moment of our lives as the sand falls through time's hourglass. We are all dying a little bit every day. Stoics repeat daily the mantra, '*memento mori*', meaning 'remember you will die' to constantly remind themselves that the gift of life is freshly renewed every day and it is something to be grateful for. We're all expiring, so let's not flatline through life but make our mark. *Memento mori* is a war cry against wasting your days. Death is not to be feared. A race, after all, is pointless without a finish line. Mortality provides us with a scorebook in which to mark our successes. We are quite literally racing against a clock. Each day you ask yourself if you're being the most productive, successful version of yourself possible.

The pack we choose to run with

'Tell me who your friends are, and I'll tell you who you are.' You are your friends or the people you choose to hang with. Groups are held together by the glue of their shared beliefs and habits, and if you want to fit in and be one of the gang you have to embrace their rituals and behaviours. The members of close-knit social groups tend to be similar in what they wear, their sense of humour, hobbies, outlook on life and income. If you lack ambition and discipline, the chances are you'll find your way to similar people who make you feel that's okay. Thankfully, I've always had great friends, positive people and killers of their own craft around me. Edward Baxter, who is now my business partner, was my most devout and valued training partner throughout my career; we pushed each other to achieve greatness every day and challenged one another to be better in and out of the pool. I remember when he was first training with me I thought, 'Who is this small kid and why has Mel asked him to come with me to Australia for seven weeks before the Olympics?' At first I was right, he struggled with the warm-up as he'd never trained in a 50m pool before. But as each day and week went by, he began getting closer and closer to me and his personality started to come out and really shine. Strangely, his thinking was scarily similar to mine. He put a huge shift in and by week seven I could safely call him one of my best friends.

As recently as 15,000 years ago we were still being hunted by superior carnivores and we lived in groups for safety in numbers. These days we still crave acceptance and membership. Humans need to be a part of a tribe in order to feel safe and will sometimes go to great lengths to fit in even if it means modifying themselves: putting on weight because the rest of the group is obese, masking good looks, or playing down our natural athleticism because it makes others feel bad. Look at gang culture: to be an accepted member you usually have to undergo incriminating rites of passage to prove your loyalty, affecting violent behaviour that is not natural to you. This fear of rejection, of being outcast if we say or do something contrary to the tribe, is something we need to break free of.

Fact: we are happier in the company of others than on our own. We were born to be social creatures, even the introverts among us – not all the time, but certainly with a balance between our outward and interior selves. Truth be told I'm a bit of a lone wolf and go my own way, I always have, but no man is an island and I have some really fine friends in my pack who are there for me at the drop of a hat and the first sign of trouble. And now with Eiri and George that pack is even stronger. You get back what you put in – that's a universal law of cause and effect. A good friendship is based on a foundation of trust, honesty and communication. The more you tend to a relationship, the more it grows. So, just as you need to invest in a comfy bed as you spend a third of your life asleep, you need to mix with those individuals who push you forward and upward, who fire you up and bring out the best of you.

There are so many factors involved in personal success, but the most important one is a strong positive mindset. It dictates how much we are prepared to suffer to get where we want, how quickly we recover from taking a knock, and the way in which we respond to everyday life and affect those around us.

Step 5: Choose the pack you run with very carefully

My pack consists of Mel Marshall, my long-time coach, the British Swimming Team, my management, my business team, close friends and most importantly, family. We must use these fellow pack members to rely on but also to lift them up at every opportunity.

Does your pack make you feel energised or drained? Do they support your purpose or try to hold you back? We need to be aware of those people around us who are energy vampires and hold us back by viewing us in the old skins of who we were. Mel always said as I was growing up, 'Be a radiator not a drain.' Individuals often find it hard to accept when one of their group outgrows them and looks further afield for new friends; they feel threatened by their friend's success because it shines a light on their *lack*. Seek out positive, self-motivated people who are upbeat, glass-half-full types, curious and active, fun-loving and encouraging. Your friends are a reflection of you and remember, the sky would be a lonely and dull place if there was only one star shining.

Chapter Six

Channelling Aggression – Harnessing Your 'Fight' Reflex

Training in Fort Lauderdale, Florida in 2019.

believe in a gladiatorial mindset. I'm ruthless with myself so why wouldn't I be ruthless with everyone else? I won't allow myself to see anyone but me on the podium because that's *my* spot, the pool is *my* realm. I'm going to do the job and I'm going to do it well. Each race I treat as a scrap, a fight in which I leave nothing but maimed egos and broken aspirations behind me in the watery arena. The roar of the crowd when you come out for a final is like nothing else. When 15,000 people are cheering for you and calling your name, it feels like you're stepping into Rome's fabled Colosseum to do battle with the very best, the adrenaline flooding and pulsing through your being like electricity, magnified by the vibrations through your feet from the sound of the crowd.

*

What you experience in life gives you a different narrative to everyone else, and like a method actor who draws on experience to help him play a role, I channel things from my past to trigger the testosterone in my body to make me stronger and faster. Shortly before a race I use moments from my past in which I felt humiliated or threatened to summon a kind of temporary internal rage. Even though I don't burst through my shirt and turn green, channelled anger for me is pure rocket fuel. I guess I have always been quite an angry young man.

Let me tell you a couple of stories about working with anger. In 2019 in Gwangju, South Korea, I was competing in the World Championships. The anger that lives inside me is like a wild animal. It bristles under my skin and makes me want to fight. When you see me pacing around before a race, my eyes hidden beneath my goggles, I feel as if I am about to go into the boxing ring. My coach Mel knows me so well. Little nuances no one else would get she sees magnified. She knew I was chomping at the bit that day of the semi-final, and a few hours before the race we went for a walk. I felt like a grenade that was about to explode, testosterone was literally coursing through me. Mel says my eyeballs were red with a kind of hunger and desire to hunt. Instead of telling me to cool my tanks, to save my energy for the following night and final, she looked at me and whispered, 'Your night is tonight, go and fucking get it.' That was the night I broke the world record and went sub-57 seconds with a time of 56.88.

As a kid I was well aware of social class, but also that families were not equal or linear within the class. I wanted my mum to drive a nice car, I wanted my parents to earn more money, I wanted to say that we had been somewhere exotic for our summer holidays rather than Wales (we should be so lucky now!). I also wanted a normal house to grow up in where we weren't worrying about money, hand me downs or feeling guilty when my mum had to fill up the car for me to go training. My mum used to say that we were living on the poverty line, but I never actually knew what she meant by that. It wasn't until 2014 when I won at the Commonwealth Games and scored my first world record that I didn't have to worry about the next pay cheque or getting my card declined when I filled my own car up.

What that inequality spawned in me as a kid was an iron determination to do well and rise above my circumstances, to make enough money so in the future my children could have everything they wanted. The anger was a raw form of ambition embedded in me by my experience of wanting more. Anger and a thirst for fairness have been within me since boyhood. I didn't have a mechanism to release these feelings of rage until later in life when, with Mel's help, I began channelling it, turning that wild energy into focused exertion. Stories of my punishing work ethic in the pool began to circulate as my name became known after the Rio Olympics in 2016. To be world champion you have to give more of yourself than the next person and I knew I had the capacity to train harder than others because of my refusal to give up. In my early teens I had an epiphany that swimming was not just a hobby but a calling, an escape.

Tapping into aggression has been a key ingredient to my success. Although you don't go nose to nose with your opponents, stare them down, trash talk or anything daft like that in swimming, at some level it is an intimidation game. While I let my thirty gold medals do the talking, behind the blank stare of my goggles something special is going on inside me. I am accessing my body's 'fight or flight' mode. But what exactly is fight or flight and how does it work?

Fight or flight

Humans are hard-wired to stay safe in the familiar rather than allow ourselves to step into the unknown. The difference between us and other animals is we have developed a higher reasoning power through a newly evolved part of the brain known as the frontal cortex. In the 4.5 billion years of the earth's existence, humanity's 140,000-year presence is barely a blink in time. As recently as 15,000 years ago humans were much lower down the food chain and still being hunted by smilodons, wolves and bears. Our survival relied on unconscious fight or flight responses hard-wired within our brains which assessed the level of threat. The oldest part of the brain, known as the amygdala or lizard brain (where our instincts are stored), is where this process takes place.

Strangely, humans have still not evolved beyond this animal state: the red mist of aggression is still very much within us – think road rage or football hooliganism – as is the ability to scarper and live another day. Chemically speaking, when the brain fancies your chances of coming out of a scrap as the winner it releases a rush of testosterone to power up your fearlessness, rage and strength. This is the *fight* response, and as women also produce testosterone, it is common to both males and females. On the other hand, if the opposition is too hard to beat, the lizard brain releases the stress hormone cortisol which propels us to escape, sharpish!

The advent of learning to cook with fire and develop weapons raised the odds in our favour and we became the apex predators. From a physiological perspective we are constantly evolving to adapt to our present environment. Now that modern twenty-first-century humans no longer require the bite power to rip at raw slabs of meat, the human jaw is getting smaller, and babies are increasingly born without wisdom teeth for the same reason. As a result of technology, we are evolving into physically weaker versions of ourselves. Apparently, our brains are also getting smaller in order to make us more placid and herd-like as a race – maybe soon we will no longer have the fight or flight response as we drift into a world where everything is done for us, where we become increasingly sedentary.

But what if we were to try and awaken the other extreme for our own benefit? What if we could consciously manipulate the *fight* response to harness that extra power for short, explosive periods of time? If our ancestors could produce their best performances because their life depended on it, then couldn't we trigger the same reaction in ourselves at choice moments and channel this natural boost of increased performance?

The Spartans

The art of channelling inner aggression is not new. Two thousand five hundred years ago, long before the gladiators of ancient Rome, the Spartans of Peloponnesian Greece were masters of this. Arguably the finest fighting force the world has ever seen, their brilliance as soldiers was built on their three core values of obedience, courage and endurance. And how they learnt to endure is the stuff of legend. Sparta hated weakness and admired strength: disabled babies were thrown off Mount Taygetus, while newborns were left overnight at the summit. If they survived the night, exposed to wild animals and cold, they had passed their first test.

A Spartan's life was one in which they were relentlessly conditioned to war. They were so attuned to fighting as a way of life that war was something they relished. Boys weren't brought up by their mothers; at the age of seven they went to live in the *agoge* with other boys where they were watched over by a warden who would encourage them to fight each other and whipped them regularly. They ate the bare minimum, walked barefoot and wore only a cloak.

If they needed something extra to eat, they were encouraged to steal it by stealth. Every year they participated in the *Diamastigosis*, a festival in which boys would be whipped voluntarily in front of the other Spartans till they bled (often to death) – it was considered an act of honour.

For all that's repulsive about them, there's a number of things we can learn from these extraordinary people in terms of approach and single-mindedness. The Spartans knew the impact their appearance had on others; dressed in a simple tunic and a long crimson cloak, they wore a gold helmet with a distinctive horsehair plume, and little armour but for greaves (shin pads). Before battle, and in view of their enemy, they would illustrate their readiness by covering themselves in oil, stretching and doing gymnastics, as well as playing musical instruments. The sight of their naked, muscled physiques alone used to scare the opposition, never mind their intimidating reputation as the world's finest warriors. But it was the steely silent confidence they exuded that their enemies found most frightening. Mothers told their sons, as wives told their husbands, 'Come back triumphant or (dead) on your shield.'

Body language

How you present yourself, not what you wear or smell like, but rather the language of your physiology, is very important. You'll never see me walk out of the ready room (where swimmers muster before a race) to my lane block with my head down, as that projects a message of weakness to my opponents, so I relax my shoulders and ensure my chin is up. I'm here for a scrap and my body needs to send a clear message to the other competitors. If I'm on my way to a competition and I'm feeling anxious and don't feel ready, I take control of myself by taking six-second breaths and six-second exhalations; these fill my brain with oxygen (one of the first results of anxiety is losing breath, which releases the cortisol stress hormone), calm me down and tell me the situation is controllable. I had learnt this from working with ex-Special Forces operatives; just before they executed a move to outmanoeuvre the enemy, they would take a few deep breaths to relax, ease anxiety and have full control of themselves when under fire.

Mike Tyson once said about his ring walks: 'I'm supremely confident but I'm scared to death, afraid of everything, afraid of losing, of being humiliated. The closer I get to the ring the more confident I get . . . Once I'm in the ring I'm a god.'

You want to relax and enjoy the moment, especially if you're doing something you've been preparing for, whether it's a triathlon or a race at the Olympic Games. You don't want to be too relaxed though, nor do you want to be overwhelmed by the enormity of the event. You need optimum performance, and the best way to summon that, I find, is through pure attack. You are here to fight – there is no such thing as defence, only attack.

Use your enemy as fuel

The story of Frenchman Henri Charrière, who in 1931 was condemned for life to the brutal penal colonies of French Guyana, is both a tragedy and a triumph. 'Papillon' as he was better known (for the tattoo of a butterfly on his chest, symbolising freedom), was found guilty of the murder of a Montmartre gangster – a crime that he didn't commit. It was three years before he escaped and hid among a leper colony, before sailing and crashing in the Gulf of Maracaibo, where he was to live for several years among a primitive tribe in the jungle.

Throughout the book he dreams of meting his own justice on the judge who sent him down, and to do this he will have to escape. What keeps him alive is the steely rage and dream of revenge that burns like a cold flame within him. He channels pure hatred and a sense of injustice and wears it like a coat; it powers him through swamps, hunger, torture, crocodile attacks; it is what keeps him going. Papillon was dipping into his red mist. Caught by French authorities he was finally interned on the infamously escape-proof Devil's Island, surrounded by shark-infested waters. His first attempt at escape meant a year in solitary confinement, the second earned him five years. Papillon wouldn't be beaten; from a cliff he watched some coconuts he had bound together get dashed on the rocks. Day by day he studied the gaps in the swell. By the time he finally escaped for good on a raft of coconuts he had made seven attempts at escape and had lost his youth. Papillon's story has become a touchstone for never giving up.

In his book *First Man In*, ex-SBS soldier Ant Middleton recounts when he was doing basic training for the Parachute Regiment and using his hatred of a fellow cadet who was bullying him to fire himself up during a running race. He passes runner after runner and finally finishes the race in first position. He is accessing his fight reflex. Middleton suggests we should think of our doubters and detractors, using their threat or what they have done to us in order to evoke fury in ourselves. Channelling anger for brief periods instantly banishes nerves and fills your body with testosterone.

In the past I have used my opponents as a breeding ground for this fuel. To me, hate can be used for good and can unlock certain doors which you would normally not have a key for. If I really wanted to beat someone then I had to make them my enemy. I love the moment in time just before the whistle goes to get on the blocks, and I can stare them down and use them to pump adrenaline through every part of me. With every second we get closer to the race I get stronger and more confident. I see the other athletes chatting away to fellow competitors in the call – or ready – room and I can never understand it. It's war and nothing less.

Summoning the red mist

While no one is going to kill me if I don't win, I find that thinking about the threat of losing and its impact on my legacy and all I have worked so hard to achieve (to name but one of my triggers) produces a quickening rage within me. What we think, we then feel.

What is it that Maximus says to his Roman soldiers in the film *Gladiator* before they face the barbarians of Germania? 'What we do in life echoes in eternity.' I've never wanted to be famous, nor do I seek adulation – I just want to create the best life for my family and burn a bright trail that will help inspire my son George to make his own mark. I believe we should be role models and set the bar high for our children and successors to strive for, and I will celebrate my son's losses as much as his wins, as failure is an integral part of the route to success. As a rage trigger I only have to think about a threat to him and picture it, and I start to feel the primal hackles rising on my back. Gradually, without succumbing to the red mist, I've taught myself how to tap into the fight response in order to power my engine to its optimum in the pool. Manipulation of this, like Wim Hof's thermo-regulation hack, is a very hard skill to come by, but accessible to almost everyone.

In our greatest challenges there can be no defence, only attack. I don't believe in going to a championship saying: 'I'm here to defend my title.' It makes no sense. The greatest conquerors in history didn't stop, they kept going, hungry to achieve more. And not just in the military but pioneers of science, sport, music and statesmen.

I've got my 'war face' on because that is what is bubbling inside of me.

Every great champion needs a nemesis

Summon too much fight and you will lose control. That we don't want. Sport is about healthy competition when two warriors meet head-on and use their skill, guile and strength to win. During the early nineties, boxers Nigel Benn and Chris Eubank were famously bitter adversaries, which made their battles in the ring great viewing. They were also equally matched – one a defensive counterpuncher, the other a toe-toe, in-your-face fighter – who brought out the best in each other and kept nothing back. One of the greatest all-round athletes ever, Daley Thompson, could never rest on his laurels so long as the West German giant Jürgen Hingsen was present. Though Daley often traded world records with him, at the major championships the double Olympic gold medallist always prevailed, if only by the narrowest of margins. Even though I manipulate hate, using it toward my opponents to power me up and beat them, it doesn't mean I wish them ill outside of the pool. Win or lose I shake hands after a race. Knowing the use and the limits of that use are very important if you want to ensure your nemesis doesn't take over and get the best of you.

My greatest rival

Since Cameron van der Burgh retired at the end of 2018, it's not really been about racing anyone else, I'm just racing myself. I miss his presence in the pool. As Cameron once said: 'You elevate yourself when you have somebody to push against. Sporting rivalries are what stories and memories are built on.'

Our rivalry was a healthy one which spurred each of us on (these days we even exchange photos of us and our babies who were born within a week of one another – who knows, one day they may be rivals!). Cameron was unpredictable. This was his strength. Knowing whether to go out fast or slow down, to go all out or hold back some energy, was tricky. Breaststroke was in a different place back then. He had great presence and an enviable pedigree; he was the Olympic champion and held multiple world records and medals. He had great arena skills too – the ability to perform on the big nights and let your strengths shine. Arena skills take years to develop; it's about knowing you can dominate the pool. Anyone can swim quick times all year round but then swim slowly at the Olympics because of the pressure.

In 2012 I raced him in Glasgow at the Commonwealth Games for the first time. These days I have no heroes as such, but it would be fair to call him my idol back then as he was the number-one breaststroker in the world. It was an honour even to be in the same race. I swam my heart out and though I was a bit intimidated I came away with gold.

That was a major turning point for me as I not only hit 58.9 seconds, one of the fastest 100m times that year, but knowing I had beaten the Olympic champ gave me so much more confidence which I took with me into the European Championships where I won four golds.

Breaking Cameron's 100m world record by half a second at the British trials in 2015 was the first time in history anyone had gone under 58 seconds for breaststroke. I thought at the time that it was quick, but I never believed it would be 57.9; I just looked at the board and thought maybe they'd got it wrong. I may have taken his world record, but Cameron wasn't giving up that easily – he was ready to take revenge and put me in my place at Kazan in Russia.

In the heats Cameron posted very quick times which I responded to:

Heat One:	Heat Two:
Van der Burgh: 58.58 secs	Van der Burgh: 58.49 secs
Peaty: 58.52 secs	Peaty: 58.18 secs

I will never forget the final of the 100m breaststroke. I thought I was winning at the turn and then I saw Cameron's feet in front of me. Van der Burgh was ahead of me all the way. With 25 metres to go I didn't think I could catch him but then my fighting spirit came through and I gave it full throttle, everything I had left in the tank. I told myself, 'Fight every inch, don't be a victim of thinking you've lost. Keep going, you can catch him.' Like a dog chasing a hare

I went for him, all my bloodlust and aggression focused on him and his feet! That final was one of the most painful and demanding races I'd yet experienced – my arms felt like they were falling off they were so leaden with fatigue – but I beat him to the touch of the wall. After that I never wanted to have such a close call again.

Controlled aggressive competitiveness can be a very positive thing. Pure rage is not. Look at when Mike Tyson, having been in jail, restarted his career and fought Evander Holyfield, ultimately losing his temper and composure and succumbing to the red mist. For those who might not know it ended up being one of the sweet science's darker moments when Tyson, frustrated and furious at being outboxed, bit off a chunk of Holyfield's ear. All was not fair in love and war. I'm glad to say they're friends now, though one of them is still missing a part of his ear.

Using music to inspire your performance

Aside of channelling aggression, I also get myself in fight mode before a race by listening to music. Music has the rare ability to lift us from our worries, stimulate our emotions and memory and help with illnesses like autism and dementia. Just hearing an old song that reminds you of a good time in your life can cheer you up; what is happening is that the song triggers memory receptors in the brain which then send you a hit of serotonin. Conversely, your mood can be ruined by a song that comes on the radio and triggers an unhappy memory. Music can also increase or decrease our heart rate, which is how I employ it in competitions.

I derive so much pleasure from music – hip hop, classical, heavy rock, dance – anything well produced, but when I'm racing, I often choose a hip-hop beat, grime or heavy rock. Powerful lyrics also send me to the moon. Before I come out for a race I never sit down, I'm on my feet pacing around with my headphones on, getting ready for the battle. The ready room is a tiny affair and when there are swimmers waiting for a relay we're cramped like sardines. I never understand how others can sit and chill – I just want to rip someone's head off. When I'm at poolside by the blocks I look to each side of my lane at my opponents and think, 'You don't deserve this, this is my race, this is my realm.' I truly believe my tribulations that have brought me to this moment give me an incredibly strong presence and self-confidence.

Music distracts us from unhelpful thoughts and the negative power of the mind. Two thousand years ago Plato, the ancient Greek philosopher, picked out certain types of music that would best motivate different professions, so they were operating in the right state. Heavy drums, he believed, were necessary for soldiers to listen to both on and off the battlefield.

The science of music

The brain has 86 billion neurons that communicate to one another through electrical pulses racing around a vast maze of dense circuitry. When they are activated, they look like a wave and therefore we call them brainwaves. The brain operates on five different frequencies that correspond to different states of thought, all of which are located in separate parts of the brain: Gamma (40–100 HZ) promotes learning, innovation, heightened perception and self-control; Beta (15–38 HZ) keeps us awake, self-aware, conscious, focused and open to learning; Alpha (7.5–12.5 HZ) relaxes us both mentally and physically, helps us be more creative and is particularly effective for sportspeople for enhancing goal setting, visualisation and *flow* states. Alpha activity also increases serotonin (feel-good) chemicals and reduces cortisol (stress hormone) release. Theta (4–7.5 HZ) helps us with meditation, insight, and the processing of new information; Delta (0.4–4 HZ) encourages deep dreaming, physical and emotional healing and rejuvenation.

I know this all sounds a bit complex if you're reading it for the first time! Brain music is a specific, frequency-based science whereby sound is produced which incorporates a specific frequency into a piece of music that has a direct effect on the listener. Like on a radio with its different bands from where each radio station emits a signal, each one of these brainwaves operates on a particular high or low frequency. The brain has a kind of tuning knob that can be turned to influence specific behaviour. By using rhythmic auditory stimulation, scientists have learnt to target specific areas of the brain and encourage certain behaviours. To translate that into plain English: by listening to certain music which operates at a certain frequency we can directly influence how awake, aggressive, calm, creative, sleepy and focused we are. Have you ever listened to a song and felt different? It's either because it stimulates a positive memory the song is associated with which immediately triggers pleasure, or because it is emitting a frequency which through neural rhythms is waking up an area of your brain which corresponds to acting in a certain way. Scientists have found that people with low gamma activity are prone to depression, impulsive and lacking in focus. They are also more vulnerable to stress.

My beats

I love the lyrics in most old school hip hop and some new era too; they're raw stories real people tell – people from the roughest areas who have risen to make the best of themselves. I love the beats, which are produced to perfection, they make you want to throw the sunroof open and roll the windows down. I grew up listening to trance with my brother Jim, who I shared a bunk bed with. We were addicted to bass, his stereo turned to the max until the next-door neighbour started hammering on the wall of our Uttoxeter semi. If my dad was in he used to thump his fist on the ceiling below and then immediately cut the power off at the switchboard, no messing. Music transports me. I love hip hop; unlike US hip hop, which feels as if it's not really going anywhere right now, in the UK, the Birmingham grime lads are stepping up – Stormy, Jaykae ... When I listen to grime and its dark undertow I *definitely* race faster. I went to a gig of Jaykae's years ago and he got me up onstage. I climbed into the mosh pit in my skinny jeans, looking like a dweeb. I love all the pushing and shoving and getting elbowed in the gut. It's a visceral expression of the music. As I've grown older my taste for music has also changed. We all have our favourite playlists and different music for certain situations, but I feel there's nothing better than relating to an artist through either success or the struggles that they may face. For me I relate to struggles, especially in my early days.

Step 6: Summoning your inner rage

Remember, the mind is the athlete, the body just does as it's told. Close your eyes and think about someone precious to you being put in harm's way or remember someone who humiliated you – you choose what gets your ire flowing – and this will trigger the first rumbles of *fight* response and change how you're feeling. Notice what is happening to you physically: clenched jaw, tensed stomach, quickened heart-beat? By becoming more aware of the physical signs we can begin to manipulate and summon that anger when we need to. Rather than summon full berserker, you need to invoke the beginning of it, let's say pink rather than maxed-out red. It will trigger the fight response in your body, and you need to control the flow of rage like a flame in a Bunsen burner. The testosterone will soon start flowing, giving you more confidence, strength and speed but like a 'power-up' on a video game it's only temporary and will leave you weary afterwards, so don't try summoning it for the whole of a marathon! This kind of energy burns like rocket fuel; it's very powerful but drains extremely quickly.

Chapter Seven

Always Be Better Than Yesterday

A few days before I flew off to my holding camp at
the Rio Olympics 2016.

Swimming is a game of chess for me, if you put the pieces in the right place you can come out with a really good or bad performance. The chase for perfection is what addicts me to the sport. One thing I always give is 110% effort. The extra 10% around the edges is what makes the difference, those little details to improve by increments. I'm obsessed with daily improvement and I get upset if I can't see myself improving. I hate stagnation. As an athlete evolves, they should be more autonomous and less reliant on their coach – it should become a fifty–fifty partnership. There are many variables that contribute to separating the supreme athlete from the ordinary one. Ultimately for me it comes down to two options when training: will this make me faster or will it make me slower?

Imagine a Formula One team constantly looking at improving their car and asking what can make it more effective, more aerodynamic, faster. When I looked at the breaststroke, I just couldn't imagine anyone getting any faster if they were to stick with that wide leg kick – something needed to change. Mel and I knew I needed to pioneer more power, but to achieve that I would require more strength, so I had to create more muscle. It's a playoff between how much muscle you have – because every centimetre of muscle means extra surface drag – so you will reach a point where you can't go any faster, and I think I'm nearing that; I'm going to get to my peak very soon. But I'm okay with that because if I can't do it, no one else can either! People say I have weaponised what was a 'dull paddle at the seaside' kind of a stroke. It's actually a massively precise stroke considered by many to be the hardest of all the four disciplines in the pool. A bit like Bartley Gorman you could say I'm the most dangerous unarmed breaststroker in the world!

Cameron van der Burgh observed of my new style: 'It's not even breaststroke any more. He's swimming like a new kind of stroke, like a metamorphosis between "fly" and "breast".' Life is about adapting and overcoming, and never allowing yourself to rest on your laurels. The day I stop looking for improvement is the day I hang my trunks up.

Listening to your body

Every season I ask myself how I can get faster, and Mel and I forensically analyse every single stroke, looking for flaws or areas we can micro-improve. In swimming, 'taper' is what we call the lead-up to a race when we take our foot off the training pedal and increase our recovery time so that our bodies are fully rested for the competition itself. When I'm in taper I become more aware of my body and exactly how it's feeling. If I've got a sore shoulder, I ask myself if I need to go and see the physio, or if it's low energy, and maybe I need more rest. If I feel a little down and negative, I know I must fix my mindset and turn it into a positive one again. Or if it's a nutrition issue and my body feels overly heavy, I might go on a light-fibre diet for the day. The thing is, the body is an extremely hard instrument to get into shape and sometimes you've got to say fuck it and just go for it no matter what.

As a professional sportsman my body is my toolkit, engine and livelihood, so it's vital I get to know all its idiosyncrasies. We need to listen to what our bodies are telling us and be vigilant as to whether it's occasionally pulling a fast one and trying to get out of doing hard work, or if there's a genuine problem that needs to be fixed. I understand my body like a car, and when the red warning light appears, I know something's wrong and how to deal with it. I'm very lucky in that my body is as strong as it is and I don't remember when I was last injured, despite lifting heavy weights and pushing myself to the extreme. When I'm racing at my best for a big race like the World Championships or the Olympics, I've prepared for so long that I know me, I know who I am and I know how to respond to myself. As they say, life is about how you respond to challenges and unexpected scenarios.

Every little push brings you closer to greatness

At the end of a training session – let's say we've done a very hard 2,000m breaststroke – Mel will always push us a little further just when we think we've finished. She'll play little mind games like: 'Anyone who wants to do a last fifty, get on the blocks.' The option to drop out is there and people do, but that's the difference between a champion who really wants it and will die for it, and someone who won't. I won't drop out even if it is my last breath. Every moment you push yourself further takes you incrementally towards greatness. If you push yourself twice a week an extra per cent, × 52, that's 104 per cent that the competition hasn't got. We train not just to win and get by, but to dominate – that's the killer instinct.

Sometimes I shout out loud to myself during training, 'Come on, you fucker, you're here for a reason!' It exposes me in front of the others – I'm putting myself on the line and that causes an adrenaline release in me. The clock never lies and sometimes at training camp we remove the clock so we are racing ourselves. When I was younger, I was highly emotional and equally competitive and when I was failing it just made me self-destruct. I had a real temper and couldn't control myself. Over time I have learnt along the road how I work and how not to do that. We change every single year and should not get obsessed with what worked for us last year as there is a good chance it will not work this year. We are constantly evolving.

*

Humans are a complex mix of hormones affected by nutrition, sleep, hydration, motivation . . . passion. On the harder days you need to find something that's going to set you apart and ensure you can step up from the level average to get the job done, to be better than yesterday. As Joe Rogan says, 'A big part of success is not being lazy and just doing it. Ninety per cent of it is just showing up.'

Always be better than yesterday

When I earned my place at the rescheduled Tokyo Olympics I was on what I called 'the home run', the most important part of the swim season - training and energy management, where I'm starting to wind down on the heavy training and to give myself a chance to recover before the Olympics. Each morning I get up and ask myself, 'How can I be better than yesterday? How can I keep pushing?' You've got to head for the optimum performance through sleep, diet, preparation, speed, power and strength training. You've got to find your battle rhythm.

Working out of McGill University in Montreal, Austrian-Canadian endocrinologist Hans Selye - also dubbed the 'father of stress research' - observed the physiological responses from a bunch of rats when subjected to an incremental increase in poison. Gradually he discovered they developed a resistance to it, whereas those given heavy doses immediately died. This ability to cope with gradual stress became known as the general adaptive syndrome or GAS.

The bottom line is that to improve at something physically you must expose your body to stress and disrupt its comfy homeostasis. That's to say, put the body through some pain, which for me means suffering the burn in my arms, gasping for breath and feeling as if my lungs are on fire and muscles are on the brink of seizing up. There is no way around this if you wish to improve and adapt.

Selye cited three stages of adaptation: alarm, resistance and exhaustion.

- The *alarm* stage – refers to the initial fight or flight reaction which is the body's natural response to stress or danger and triggers either the production of cortisol to *flee*, or the release of testosterone to *fight*.
- The *resistance* phase – comes after the initial shock of the alarm phase when the higher blood pressure lowers, and the heart rate drops. If the stress is not resolved then the body is still on alert and begins to adapt to living with higher stress hormones, making you frustrated and irritable.
- The *exhaustion* phase – think chronic stress and burnout, where both in your body and mind you no longer think or perform well. Cue depression, anxiety, chronic fatigue and a weaker immune system.

I know only too well when I've overtrained. Those days my body doesn't have the spark to lift weights or race to its fullest and I feel flat and tired before I've even put my trunks on. That's because my homeostasis is out of whack and I've overstressed my body – rather like the rats who were not given a gradually increased dosage of poison, but a big dose and died straight away. Without being given the time to repair themselves the mind and body will break down. So, when I've overtrained, I give my body the time it needs to rest and replenish. That day in April before trials for the Olympics I had my first breakdown. The journey to reach this point had been so exhausting and I felt all of my spiritual, physical energy utterly depleted. I still turned up to training and swam every lap I was tasked with but with every length I kept asking myself why now wasn't a good time to retire? I had had enough. Afterwards I talked to Mel and on the way home I cried with sheer exhaustion. The glory and the victory can sometimes seem so far away, but remember, every day the sun rises and sets, we never know what the next day will bring. Having gotten steaming with my best mate Ed the following night I felt like a different person the next day; it was as if a hole had been bored in my skull and was letting all the clogged-up pressure out, like when you bleed a radiator. I felt happy again.

Defeat develops you

The moment you get cocky and think you know it all is when you expose yourself to a loss. Sometimes you need a hit of reality, a defeat, to make you appreciate winning, as *only* winning can become numb. Also, success is certainly sweeter if you have tasted failure along the way. A champion should be forged on the fire of failure and resilience: every time you're knocked down, you pick yourself back up and on you go.

One defeat was more than enough for me, and to ensure it didn't happen again – *ever* – I channelled my anger from it to help myself rebuild and improve. Anger when tempered is brilliant fuel for high performance. To come back stronger we changed my style – at the Commonwealth Games I'd lost too much weight through a different approach to nutrition, so come race time I was too light and my focus was somewhere else. I lost my killer instinct and drive. As many professional boxers will know, if you cut too much weight too fast your strength and testosterone suffers. So, for the European Championships I put the weight back on, followed our original approach and broke the world record with a slight attitude of fuck it, I've got nothing to lose!

Since that dark day of defeat, I've managed to push myself ever further into what others consider to be impossible territory. 'Impossible' is a good place to be – there are no set rules, and you get to rewrite the script. Once upon a time, people thought the world was flat, until it was proved it wasn't. Sometimes you need to break free of the herd, the naysayers who deem it can't be done, and ask yourself which of your beliefs or those of other people are holding you back from all that you can be. You've got to be completely honest with yourself. Even if you are having a bad day of it, you have to aim to always be better than yesterday.

Basketball hero Kobe Bryant, who sadly passed away in 2020, had an inspiring take on self-improvement: 'Everything was done to try and learn how to become a better player. Everything. So when you have that point of view then literally the world becomes your library because to help you become better at your craft ... because you know what you want, the world is giving you exactly the information 100% you need because you know what you're looking for.' Bryant said we should be honest about our strengths and weaknesses. 'I was quick but not insanely quick, so I had to rely on skills a lot more, I had to rely on angles a lot more, study the game.'

Admit what is going wrong, then focus on making your weaknesses stronger.

Take away the need

The beliefs we hold about ourselves directly enable or impede our best performance. And if we put external pressures on ourselves, it will only increase the burden. As they get older athletes acquire mortgages, cars, children and expensive things to pay for, and so end up putting more pressure on themselves and their performance for the wrong reason. They no longer *want* to win for the sake of winning, they *need* to win to pay for all their acquisitions. This is an unhealthy place to operate from. Need.

Bryan Cranston, the acclaimed actor from *Breaking Bad*, a series I rate, tells an interesting story about need. Twenty-five years ago he couldn't catch a cold, never mind a break. But then he had an epiphany, as something shifted in his thinking which changed his professional life for the better, and he went from blowing opportunities at auditions to being one of the most sought-after actors in Hollywood. Actors live an up-and-down existence: even when they are working they are prone to worrying about where their next gig is coming from. If it's been a while since their last job, they unintentionally take their money worries into meetings with them. As Cranston says: 'When you put yourself in a position of need you relinquish power and control over to some unknown entity . . . I can tell in a second when there is need, it just leaks out and nobody wants to hire somebody who desperately needs a job, they want to hire people who are confident in themselves.' Cranston's new approach was to enjoy the audition for what it was: a place where he served the script and helped tell the story. Worrying about money was not helping.

I want and enjoy success that brings money to me in abundance so I can take care of my family; its sole purpose is to make life a little easier. It's nice to have enough so you don't have to worry about it, and I think having a childhood in which we had very little had pushed me to make damn sure that I never find myself in that position again. However, money without a deep happiness of your home, family and life has little value. We can't take it with us but it does help us do things which can create amazing memories and experiences.

Step 7: Finessing your process to reach your goal

How can you improve on where you are now? What have other people tried? Can you refine or finesse any of your process? Make a list of ten things that are currently working to help you achieve your goal. Now write the same things in order of which are working best. How can you improve the last five things?

Chapter Eight

Bouncing Back When Things Go Wrong

Me, my Mum & Nan at the 2017 World Championships in Budapest.

One of the reasons I love to fail is because the bounce-back is so rewarding, even though I might be in extreme physical or mental pain. Stoics had this nailed to a tee as they believed they could learn to endure pain without showing their feelings or complaining. It was also about planning for things to go wrong in the future so they could really master and focus on the present. By identifying possible problems on the road ahead, they would figure the best way to deal with each one. That's not to say they spent the present worrying about the future; it was quite the opposite: by considering the possibilities of what could throw them off their daily course – and how each one could be mitigated or removed – they were able to live more in the present than if they were to just leave themselves open to chance misfortune.

Seneca, a Roman slave and one of the great Stoics, said: 'What is unlooked for is more crushing in its effect, and unexpectedness adds to the weight of a disaster. This is a reason for ensuring nothing ever takes us by surprise. We should project our thoughts ahead of us at every turn ... rehearse them in your mind: exile, torture, war, shipwreck. All the terms of our human lot should be before our eyes.'

These days NASA employs the same rationale with their astronauts – they sweat the small stuff and prepare for everything that might go wrong in space, so when the shit does hit the fan, the astronaut won't blow his cool and will have a better chance of solving the problem having already rehearsed for it. By anticipating curveballs, we are psychologically more prepped, we've got time to raise a defence or avoid the problem if possible; that's not to say run away, but if trouble can be avoided then we should use that precious energy for something good. Forewarned is always forearmed. Planning helps us be more resistant to hardship in the knowledge that life always has the power to take away who or what we love at any moment.

By regularly looking ahead and planning for curveballs, we can learn to be grateful for those closest to us and better appreciate what we have worked hard for. If your parents are getting old, the truth is they will pass sooner than later. You can blindly ignore this and pretend they will just keep going forever, or you can prepare yourself for that inevitability; just by thinking of them not being there you stop taking them for granted and start making the most of them. This in turn increases your capacity for gratitude. Some call this process *negative visualisation* – imagining the worst so you can appreciate the best.

I find that the more prepared I can be, the more I can enjoy the race, and flourish. I also find that having made a list of things I can and can't change frees up my mental bandwidth so I can focus on the more important things. Worrying gets us nowhere.

It's not what is thrown at you but how you deal with it that counts

When we think about the things that keep us awake at night– losing our job, getting cancer, our kids' grades at school – how many of these things can we control? The answer is very few, for while you can get health insurance you have no control over the spread of cancer, and while you can influence your boss it is they who ultimately have control of whether you keep or lose your job. Epictetus made two lists: the first was 'things within our control', the second was 'things beyond our control'. While things we can't control included: the past, the future, parents, friends, illness, weather and death; under things within our control he just wrote one word: 'belief'. We are free to choose what we believe and therefore how we react to any given situation.

When we accept that we can't control others' reaction to us, just the way we react to them, it gives us a certain freedom and takes away a great many worries that we have no influence over. We do have dominion over our responses. We can let situations overwhelm us or we can rise above them. Earlier, I mentioned Kazan in 2015 when the British swim team went to Russia for the World Championships, but let me give you a bit more detail of what we had to deal with.

We were travelling for a whole day only to arrive exhausted at the rooms supplied by the host because we had to fly via Istanbul and then it took another few hours to get accredited. Unbelievably, there were no curtains or blinds in the bedrooms, which meant we wouldn't be able to sleep properly and rest up before we raced because of the unremitting sunlight. The food was absolutely disgusting. Rather than react and rise to the situation at hand, we improvised blackout blinds and I survived on granola bars. And though I could have let it get to me, I buried any contempt by enjoying the place. What a fascinating place Kazan is, with its remnant Soviet buildings and their brutalist-style architecture. I'm fascinated by the cold war period of history, the sheer vastness of the USSR, the space race with the U.S., the new technology and then when it all came tumbling down with Glasnost and perestroika, as the once mighty Soviet bear lost so many of its territories. The arena we raced in was absolutely stunning.

I wasn't going to give the situation the satisfaction of besting me. Despite Cameron van der Burgh being on red-hot form, I won, going under 58 seconds for the first time ever.

On another occasion – much more recently, in 2021 – I was in Budapest for six weeks for the ISL (International

Swimming League). Training had been going well but in the first three rounds of the heats I was swimming slow times and I wasn't dominating the way I was used to doing. I was new to being a father, and little George, my baby son, had been keeping me and my partner awake throughout the night with his crying and constant nappy changes. I was on the backfoot before I even got to Budapest! The first four weeks were the preliminary heats and we had to stay on Margaret Island, a little patch of land between Buda and Pest; the two halves separated by the Danube river which make up the city of Budapest. There was nothing stimulating to do on the island and my energy sunk the more bored I became. In week four I caught food poisoning from some dodgy chicken and the next three days were spent close to the porcelain throne with constant diarrhoea. I pulled out of my heat feeling thoroughly miserable. It wasn't looking promising.

I managed to turn it round in a week from being a belea-guered beat-up victim to breaking a new world record. This happened because I made a much-needed decision to chill. Jimmy Guy, one of my teammates since 2012, came to my room and we had a few beers, some fast food and listened to an artist called Blade. Again like that dreaded day in April when I broke down but then loosened off with a few beers being normal, I woke up the next day feeling renewed, as if I had let all the toxicity out via a secret valve. Sometimes you just need to let go and reset your thinking, be a normal human being doing what normal people do. I think just having a beer and relaxing put me in a different headspace. We put too much pressure on ourselves to continually work and be focused; sometimes you need to just take yourself away from it all for a little while.

I have a completely dominant mindset that says: 'I'm going to make this happen no matter what.' When you create this unstoppable force in your mind and body, even when you are tired, you are still capable of finding your best-ever performance. Sometimes you just need to blow off steam before you get back on the horse, and sometimes you have to grit your teeth and make the best of a bad lot.

Resilience

Resilience derives from the ancient Latin word *resilio*, meaning to bounce back into shape. It's a very topical word at the moment, especially after so many of us found ourselves to be quite the opposite of resilient during the global lockdown that went with Covid-19. While other countries with looser restrictions allowed their athletes to go on swimming camps we had no such option, and I decided I could either moan about it or create my own regime in the garage with weights, or keep fit on my bike.

Covid-19 presented so many challenges to everyone, not least those poor families who lost their livelihoods. Resilience at our deepest low is sometimes hard to find, it may feel like you're literally searching for a needle in a haystack. I struggled through that whole period because I felt I had nothing to look forward to, no competitions that were definitely going ahead so I ate a lot of junk food, drank a lot of alcohol and binged on Netflix. But despite this I still had the ability to summon resilience and every day I cycled 40kms, swam three hours in my spa pool, and lifted weights three times per week. I put on 10kg of muscle.

At Sandhurst Military Academy, future British Army officers learn that just because an exercise might have gone wrong in the morning there's no point dwelling on it and feeling useless for the rest of the day, as that kind of energy will be taken into your next task and taint it. Your day is not one long continuum but is made up of hundreds of micro moments which means you have the power to flex your behaviour at any time and start afresh. If I have a disappointing training session that makes me feel shit, I have two choices: I can just leave it there at the pool and resolve that tomorrow will be better, or I can take it back home with me and let it infect the rest of my day and the moods of those closest to me. I have the choice.

Winning once is easy but to sustain first place over several years is much more difficult. Going into Rio '16 my mindset was only about beating the world record and winning the gold. Afterwards, there was the inevitable post-Olympic blues and a period that was spent readjusting and recalibrating what my next goal was going to be. Thereafter, I was cruising through life very happily until I was beaten at the 2018 Commonwealth Games. It was the just the shock I needed. There is nothing wrong with failing when you're on the road of learning – you get to know yourselves better in defeat than when you're winning all the time. Having to go back to the drawing board and taking a fresh perspective is a healthy thing as it challenges us and makes us grow. I was beaten because I'd lost too much weight following a different approach to nutrition, so come race time I'd been too light and my focus was somewhere else; this time I put the weight back on, followed our original approach and won the world record three months later. Success is so much sweeter if you have tasted failure along the way.

Resilience is picking yourself back up every time you're knocked down, brushing yourself off, remembering your why and then going for it. My coach Mel believes you shouldn't get lost in the highs and lows, thinking too much about winning and too much about losing. Obviously hard work is a given – you're not going to get anywhere in this world without being utterly dedicated to your chosen path. For me it's a relentless pursuit of excellence. You see me on the TV for perhaps a minute and yet it takes four years training to get to that minute.

Growing through experience

In 2013, I just missed qualifying for the World Championships by 0.03 seconds. In 2014, fed up with coming second or third and missing getting on the team, I switched up a gear. I wanted to be that guy who was making the finals and winning medals, and ever since that decision I've broken a world record every single year. As a child swimmer and young adult, I'd be shitting bricks a week before a swimming event. Nowadays, through experience, I've developed what we call 'arena skills', the ability to take the crowds and pressure in my stride. And besides, I'm so busy that I barely have time to worry about what happens outside of today. It's all a journey.

Each experience you survive that you were worried about makes you grow as a person. When you challenge yourself to push through fears, you soon realise their scare factor was created by the negative monkey chatter in your head. With a can-do attitude your life changes to one of limitless adventures rather than a timid, predictable existence where you sleepwalk through your days. It's not the days which are to blame, it's us. We only grow when we are prepared to take a risk and push ourselves outside our comfort zone. Little steps create big progress.

Comfort zones

The anthropologist Joseph Campbell in his book *Pathways to Bliss* says our hero's journey begins in the darkest part of the forest where there are no paths laid down by others for us to follow. We must have faith in ourselves, step into the unknown and break free of the comfort zone which has enchained us. A comfort zone is a complete misnomer as it is not comfortable at all, it's just a place where you tread water but you're not happy or fulfilled. The fear of the unknown holds us back and keeps us from achieving our true potential. Life is truth; by the time it's over, isn't it our aim to have found out who we are? Ollie Ollerton says: 'We should embrace short-term discomfort for long-term gain. However, we are hard-wired to take short-term comfort, and this leads to long-term pain.'

Rewiring our thinking of the last 200,000 years starts by recognising your reluctance to take the path untrodden, but then knowing it is the only way forward if you are to make meaningful change. What's that old saying? 'Feel the fear and do it anyway.' Humans are at their best when we are in pursuit of something, when we test ourselves and take calculated risks. We all have areas in our life where we know we could make improvements but instead we often think, 'If it's not broke, don't fix it,' or 'I'll do it next week,' until suddenly years have passed by and it's too late, there are no more *next weeks*.

It's not enough to just turn up for life, we need to push

ourselves to where we have never been. Goggins has this to say about our pampered existence being counterproductive: 'You are in danger of living a life so comfortable and soft that you will die without ever realising your potential,' but, 'If you're willing to suffer, and I mean suffer, your brain and body once connected together, can do anything.'

Voluntary discomfort

Have you ever heard of voluntary discomfort? Coined by the Stoics of ancient Greece, it's a term that describes placing yourself in hardship from time to time in order to learn resilience and to stretch your physical and mental boundaries. The philosophers of that time were not just a bunch of dry academics who sat in a room theorising and conversing: Socrates was the toughest soldier in the Athenian army; Plato, his star student, was a famous wrestler; while Cleanthes the Stoic was a boxer. The Stoic student regularly exposes themself to hardship, be it heat, cold, hunger, simple food, strenuous exercise or sleeping on a hard bed. Through this the body becomes tough, the soul enduring and strong.

Every year, Mel made sure the Derby swim team went somewhere different for our training camps, and one year in particular – back in 2013 – we went to Zambia in Central Africa. Now Zambia, despite having one of the best wildlife parks on the continent and lovely, friendly people, is not the first choice for a swimming training camp. Looking back,

Mel obviously wanted us to be uncomfortable. She wanted us to have a dose of *voluntary discomfort*.

We arrived at the accommodation thoroughly knackered after a long flight and discovered there was no Wi-Fi, no kind of home comforts whatsoever. I could hear the cockroaches in the skirting boards in my room, and there was no fridge to keep the milk cool for breakfast. It was a joke. The next morning, minus the cereal and cold milk in our tums, we turn up at the pool and there's no one to open the gates. The place is deserted, so we end up having to shimmy over these colossal ten-foot gates. If that isn't a bad enough start to the day, we then see the pool we are to train in for the next week. 'For fuck's sake,' I say, 'it's bright green!' The last time it tasted chlorine was anybody's guess – certainly not this century.

It was extremely unsafe, but weirdly Mel was just like, 'Right, just go, this is the warm-up, this is the training camp.' Not surprisingly, halfway through I became severely ill and I had to stop training for a bit. It was a massive learning curve for me; there is always wisdom which can be learnt in discomfort, and this was a lesson in resilience. By putting myself out there I made the best of the situation, and I enjoyed it. It was also a lesson in contrast, as it created a sense of gratitude for the next training camp we went to, which had all the comforts you could ask for. We wouldn't have appreciated them half as much if we hadn't experienced the flip side of the coin in Zambia. You have to make the most of difficult situations.

Look for positives in a negative situation

I think it's about *how* you respond to challenges day to day that forms who you are in life. You can stand there whining about your lot or you can throw yourself into making the best of things. If you cultivate an upbeat attitude where you try to look for a positive in any negative situation, you are more likely to find valuable nuggets of wisdom along the way and live a happier life. If you treat every day with curiosity and enthusiasm rather than with a sense of fear, or boredom, life begins to sparkle with possibility and doors open that weren't previously there. Our true inner self is one that welcomes adventure and that feels happiest when its wings are stretched.

Two thousand years ago, Epictetus said: 'When a difficulty falls upon you, remember that God, like a trainer of wrestlers, has matched you with a rough man. "For what purpose?" you may say. Why, that you become an Olympic conqueror.' I think hard times can be good for us, they shape us. Unless you experience the worst of the worst you won't ever appreciate the best as you will have nothing to compare it to. That's one of the reasons I love travel; it can be tough, and things can go wrong when you're out of your comfort zone in a strange land. Sometimes you have to leave and travel far across the world to realise what treasures lie waiting for you at home. St Augustine once said: 'The world is a book and those who do not travel read only one page.'

Be prepared for things to go wrong and be ready to embrace them with a determined smile. The only way to develop a tough, resilient mindset is by competing with yourself. If early mornings are not your thing, it's about pushing yourself out of bed *earlier* than you normally would.

The fatigue triangle

There are three types of fatigue: mental, physical and spiritual. Are you mentally exhausted because you have been working long hours hunched over a computer without breaks and your brain feels like it's had the life sucked out of it? Are you physically shot because you have been training? Perhaps you feel spiritually drained, maybe you've lost your purpose or no longer believe in what you are doing?

Energy is like a bike tyre, and when you feel deflated the sooner you locate the puncture that has drained away your energy, the sooner you know *what* to rest. Your body will tell you, as will your mind or soul. Getting to know your emotions and learning how you tick is essential to leading a happy, fulfilled life and to success in general. When we become more self-aware we become more mindful of the effect our state is having on ourselves and the people around us.

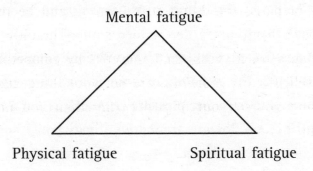

Mental fatigue

Physical fatigue   Spiritual fatigue

Mental fatigue

Whatever we are focusing on achieving, be it completing a degree, trying for a promotion, writing a book or training for a marathon, there's a finite amount of daily energy we can throw at it. Energy can be sapped as a result of stress, the pressures of work, parenting, supporting a family, dealing with an ongoing illness – there are loads of reasons. If you find your head is cloudy and you can't process things as quickly as normal, it's probably because you need some headspace. Are you taking too much on and afraid of saying *no* to others? Time to take a break and rest your mind.

When you hit a mental wall, try and remove yourself from it; standing there looking at a computer screen won't do any good. Taking yourself away from whatever is blocking you and enjoying something different is important. Reset your mind by tuning into something else that stimulates you, whether it's as simple as taking a walk outside or relaxing mentally. Personally, I love to switch things up by spending time with my son.

Perhaps you need to insert exercise into your daily routine. Taken in the morning, exercise is a great energiser as it releases serotonin, the pleasure chemical, as a reward and gets your blood flowing around your body which increases your alertness. It also gives you some 'you time'. When we exercise, we create a respectful dialogue with our body and position ourselves for improved mental health. Exercise gives you mental space because it can take you out of your immediate environment.

Physical fatigue

As we saw in the chapter on pain, your physical fatigue could be a result of your body going into flight mode as you may be attempting to do something new, or it may be the case that you've trained like a boss and your body is simply aching and crying out for a rest. If you start the day with no energy despite the fact you've had a good night's sleep, perhaps it could be you've lost your spark and need a new sense of purpose. Remember that we all need our *ikigai*, a reason to get up in the morning. If you don't feel your fire is burning with a strong enough glow, get yourself to the doctor's for a check-up – you may be anaemic or deficient in a particular vitamin. There are many debilitating conditions that might be leeching your physical energy: diabetes, glandular fever, shingles, ME . . . so go and get a body MOT. One of the most important but overused sayings is 'you are what you eat'. I feel anxious when my diet is poor, or my energy the next day is inconsistent. It might sound boring but you have to try and find a balance. Nutritious food can unlock so much more of our physical and mental energy and conquer fatigue.

Spiritual fatigue

This is more serious as it hints at an existential crisis – when we feel like our purpose is no longer propelling us towards joy, or when nothing makes sense any more and we lose belief in ourselves. Sometimes the joy goes out of what you do. You may ask yourself, what is the point of all this effort for something I no longer believe in, and would anyone care if I stopped doing what I do? Would they even notice?

Spiritual fatigue is when your soul is weary and can present itself as a mixture of all three. It might be your inner self crying out for a vital and necessary change. When we become spiritually bankrupt it's because we have lost belief in ourselves or someone close to us. We feel hollow and uninspired. As I mentioned earlier, in 2020 I came unstuck. And while my swimming training was going well and my body was fine, my mind was completely exhausted. We often think getting rest is about lying down on the sofa or grabbing an early night, but that's for physical fatigue; resting your mind can sometimes mean doing the opposite of rest – in other words stimulating your brain through doing something you love doing or trying something new.

I found myself thinking soul-destroying, self-sabotaging thoughts of retiring. I had been pushing my body so hard and taking things so seriously that I had reached breaking point. One morning, I found myself in tears at the wheel of my car. Instead of training that afternoon I went for a walk with Ed followed by a damn good drink with him. In times of spiritual burnout people are our best anchor – without them, and left alone, we are vulnerable to negative mind chatter.

Lazy brains

The problem with our brains, as we know, is they take shortcuts, presenting us with automatic responses; in this autopiloted, low-battery mode you feel bored, uninspired and unmotivated. This makes me think of the movie *Soul*, which reminds us that we should slow down to start living and stop focusing on how we will feel in the future: 'When I'm wealthy, world champion, married etc. . . . only then will I feel complete.' *Soul*'s main character, Joe, is a musician and has spent his life believing that only after performing in a jazz quartet will he feel complete; for now, his life as a teacher is redundant. But then he learns that there's a difference between purpose and joy and that every moment is to be lived. If you can find your spark, doing that which makes you happy, you're on the right track.

I had been trying to keep on top of my training during the pandemic, as well as moving house and having a new baby, on top of which I was running the business and dealing with the sponsors and commercial opportunities. I guess I was juggling too many plates and was burning out as I wasn't taking any time for myself. Life doesn't have to be serious *all* the time, and by stopping and taking stock of how I was feeling I realised the thing I needed most was some *lightness*. I had a couple of glasses of wine at a friend's house and had a lovely evening. Just this simple change of environment was all I needed to blow a few cobwebs away, to hear myself laugh again and reset. A life lived well is not only full of focus but full of laughter too. Sometimes, when I do relax over a glass of something alcoholic in a pub, I'll get a raised eyebrow and someone's expression will say: 'You can't have a drink, you're an athlete,' which really irks me. I'm a human being, I'm not public property, nor am I any less flawed than anyone else. It might be a light-hearted joke but small remarks like that make people guilty for something that should be completely normal.

It's so important to talk to someone when you're feeling low as by not sharing it you are carrying a heavier load than you need to, one that infects you and darkens your days. The longer you leave it the heavier it gets. Look at the U.S., where healthcare must be paid for and only a few can afford it. Young men without access to therapy, who have never been taught any emotional awareness by their parents, have become increasingly angry and isolated from society; the next thing we know is they end up expressing that disaffection by massacring innocents in the local mall or school. Sharing how you're feeling with someone you trust is like lancing a boil and letting all the toxic pressure out. Don't give it even the slightest chance to become a boil.

To nip burnout (and the depression that comes with it) in the bud, you need to check in with yourself every day. Ask yourself each morning, how am I feeling? But not first thing in the morning – you need to get yourself out of bed first as your thoughts will try to keep you in there, telling you all sorts of nonsense. Mel Robbins, author and creator of *The 5 Second Rule*, says we have about five seconds when we first wake up before our negative thoughts kick in. So as soon as your alarm goes you've got to rocket out of bed and meet the day, rather than hitting snooze and letting the day come to you.

Step 8: Facing fears

When you pin down the things/situations/people you're afraid of and make a list of them, you may find there are fewer things than you thought. Go for the top fear and focus on what you feel when you think about it. Where is it on a scale of one to ten, if one is low-level fear and ten is red alert? If it's a fear of water – which, by the way, I suffered as a kid to the extent I didn't want to go in the bath – go and spend some time in your local pool, your nearest wild-swimming lake or the sea. Get familiar with water by little increments: dip a toe, then a leg and gradually immerse yourself. As your brain starts to realise it's not going to hurt you, you will begin to form a very different relationship with it.

Chapter Nine

No Substitute for Hard Work – Graft vs Talent

My lunch break on my AP Race Clinics. Exhausted!

Gladiators had to be ultra-fit and at the top of their game every time they stepped onto the hallowed sand of Rome's Colosseum. Some of the most celebrated gladiators garnered a level of fame comparable to today's rock star or A-list actor, and were so valuable to their owners that they only fought once or twice a year. To achieve this level of celebrity they worked at their craft behind the scenes, so that on the day they could shine as brightly as their golden breastplates and shimmering weapons. They made their swordplay or trident throwing look easy, but every defensive and offensive move had to be practised again and again before it became embedded in the gladiator's mind. They were not born fighters, but the product of thousands of hours of training. The same happens in sport; an athlete is slowly moulded over time, their mindset developed, their strengths built upon, and their weaknesses overcome. Nothing happens overnight.

Imagine an iceberg poking from the sea: when a gladiator or modern-day athlete performs you are only seeing the tip of the iceberg though there's so much more supporting it under the surface. If you see me racing on TV for perhaps a minute (hopefully it's at least four seconds less than that if I'm doing the 100m!) it's over so quickly and yet that single revolution of the second hand on the clock has taken four years of hard graft to accomplish. The same can be said of the 100m sprint in athletics. Technique in explosive short events is crucial, as there's no margin for error.

A load of bull

After months of conditioning, strength and speed preparation, on the day there's a number of things I need to keep an eye on: rapid reaction time off the blocks, a long underwater pullout, following the streamline created by my pull for as long as possible, stroke precision – keeping to a strong narrow kick followed by a wide pull – maintaining a high body position in the water, a low stroke count and a good turn. All are integral to winning and anything can go wrong. The pursuit of excellence is achieved by relentless practice.

A story goes that Picasso, arguably the most important artist of the last century, was approached by a tourist who kept pestering him for a sketch. Picasso complied with a quick flourish of his pen and drew a bull. 'You owe me $10,000,' he said flatly. The tourist baulked. 'Why? It only took you thirty seconds to do.' The artist looked at him squarely. 'Wrong, it took me forty years to do that.' You don't get the end product without putting the time in. It might involve a thousand steps to get where you want to go, but by focusing on the smaller details the overall goal comes to you in the end.

If I've broken a world record and post it on social media, my critics are quick to claim that I just 'got lucky', but there is no such thing as sustained, regular luck. Winning the lottery twice, now that's lucky, but if someone is consistently winning at sport there is something more dependable at work behind their success – it's called graft, and it separates the boys from the men, and the committed from the half-hearted. Trollers are insecure and jealous people; it's easier for them to dismiss someone's hard work than create their own achievements. I wouldn't walk into a Wall Street bank and say to a trader, 'You've got to where you are by pure luck.' In a normal nine-to-five job, I could slip up one day and make up for it the next, but with my profession we don't have that luxury – screw up at the Olympics and you have to wait another four years to silence your demons.

You have to really want it

How far do you think natural talent alone will take you? Go down to your local swimming club and look at a bunch of youngsters swimming, and you can easily see which kids have got potential to be good. However, to become great, to go *all* the way, there are so many variables that need to come into play beyond mere talent. In his book, *Bounce: The Myth of Talent and Power of Practice*, Matthew Syed nails down some of the keys to his success as a former British number-one table tennis player, asserting that had certain key conditions not been met, his achievement would never have occurred:

- He had a full-size table tennis kit in the garage.
- He had a competitive brother who he could play table tennis with and amass thousands of hours of practice.
- Peter Charters, his school sports coach, was the number one table tennis coach and scout for the English Table Tennis Association.
- He was able to train 24/7 at the Omega club, a table tennis club with a number of national-level players.

Malcolm Gladwell, in his book *Outliers*, echoes this: 'The people who stand before kings may look like they did it all themselves. But in fact they are invariably the beneficiaries of hidden advantages and extraordinary opportunities and cultural legacies that allow them to learn and work hard and make sense of the world in ways others cannot.'

Is there such a thing as natural talent in professional sport? Of course. But I also think the pathway to excellence and success in any given field depends upon very specific key factors: having the correct mindset, absolute self-discipline, genetic advantage (if it's sport), the right teacher, access to the right kit, selfless parents to support you and a personal hunger for success. Remove one or two of these vital building blocks and the chances of success grow dimmer very quickly. Take the need for a supportive family and having the right coach: if I hadn't been spotted by Mel as a young lad I wouldn't be swimming now, I'd probably be a brickie or in the forces. And if I hadn't had a mum who was prepared to drive me, even if I *had* met Mel, I couldn't have physically got to the poolside for 4.20 a.m.

Inner drive is the most vital asset for success; if you don't want it badly enough you won't see the point in suffering the hardships en route to your goal. And it's the hardships you suffer that create resilience, wisdom and strength. David Beckham is often cited as an example of someone who was obsessively driven in their practice. To nail those perfect penalty crosses he became famous for, you have to rewind to him as a little boy, kicking a ball at a precise spot on a wall, over and over again, whatever the weather. Daley Thompson, regarded as one the greatest decathletes ever, was renowned for training harder and longer than anyone else. Other British athletes tell many a story of their calling it a day come dusk, while Thompson would still be out in the dark on his own under the floodlights, working on his weakest disciplines. Champions in life and sport get there because they have the hunger to better themselves and the discipline to see it through. Talented youngsters without discipline might make it to club level but rarely any further.

When we talk of natural talent, be it Muhammad Ali or Lewis Hamilton, to reach that level of proficiency they had to develop their raw talent over thousands of hours of practice. It has been suggested that to become an expert in anything takes at least ten years or ten thousand hours of application. What many of us don't realise about Ali, for example, is that before he turned professional and wowed the world when he felled Sonny Liston, he had already fought over a hundred amateur fights and been a national Golden Gloves champion. There's no such thing as an overnight success. While his formidable hand speed was natural, his ability to read his opponent and direct the fight – we call it 'ring smarts' or 'boxing IQ' – wasn't congenital at all, but the sum total of his experience in the ring over a long period of time.

In 2014, aged twenty-three, Lewis Hamilton became the youngest racing driver ever to win a Formula One World Championship, as well as being the first black driver to race in the sport. He holds more wins than any other driver in the history of the sport and has been the Formula One world champion a record seven times. His first F1 win was in 2008, but to understand the time that was put in to get to this point we have to rewind to 1993 when, aged eight, he started competitive karting. Two years later he won the British cadet karting championship. That same year when he was getting the autograph of Ron Dennis, the team boss at McLaren F1, he introduced himself and said, 'One day I want to be racing your cars.' Along with his signature Dennis wrote, 'Phone me in nine years and we'll sort something out.' Hamilton made his F1 debut in 2007. It took thirteen years for him to rise from British cadet champ to world champ. Again, a parent played a massive part in his ascendancy to greatness – his father, Anthony, sometimes held up to four jobs to support his son's ambition.

Genetic advantage

Certain people, thanks to their build, physiology and geographical environment, are more naturally suited to some sports than others. For instance, when it comes to mountain climbing, a person born at high altitude will be more suited to it than somebody born at sea level. The Nepalese people have evolved to be at home in the thin air of the Himalayas, their bodies able to produce more haemoglobin which carries oxygen in the blood. In the same way as the Inuit people in the Siberian and North American Arctic have genetically evolved to tolerate a fat-dominated diet due to the animals they feed on. Twenty thousand years ago, according to the University of California, genetic mutations occurred which limit the height and weight of the Inuit and allow them to function better on a diet rich in omega-3s.

The Bajau people are nomads who live on boats in the waters of the Philippines, Malaysia and Indonesia. They hunt for fish on the seabed and can hold their breath for up to an astonishing thirteen minutes. It's been established marine animals who spend a lot of their life underwater have larger spleens. Using saliva kits and a portable ultrasound machine, Melissa Lardo (from the Centre for GeoGenetics at the University of Copenhagen) was able to measure the spleens of Bajau people and discovered they were dispro-portionately larger than those of non-Bajau people living on the Indonesian mainland.

When it comes to sport, some of us are seemingly built by the gods for a specific event. Michael Phelps, winner of twenty-three Olympic gold medals and the first swimmer to earn a place on five Olympic teams, has huge size-14 feet, paddle-like hands and not only hyper-extended joints but double-jointed ankles which allow him to bend them 15 per cent more than the average swimmer; added to which he has a longer than usual wingspan and a very long torso and short legs. His chest is also hyper-jointed so he has more force driving his kick with each stroke. And if that isn't enough, Poseidon gifted him one more weapon: his body produces half the lactic acid (a chemical formed as a result of prolonged exertion that forces the body to stop and recover) than the rest of us, which allows him to go longer at full tilt without his muscles seizing up.

As a swimmer I have a certain amount of genetic advan-tage. I come from a long line of big men. My dad's big, though he's never been to a gym in his life, while on my mum's side we are tall. I've got large shoulders, size-12 feet and huge shovels for hands which help me plough through the water. And then there's the fact that I am hyper-jointed.

I have the ability to extend my shin away from my knee. Mel says my feet are on backwards because my knees and my feet are double-jointed which allows me to kick with great force but still keep my stroke narrow and streamlined without inviting much resistance from the water. This is a massive advantage, but without the endless hours of hard work I put in at the pool these physical bonuses are useless.

Tyson Fury has larger lungs than the average person – obviously he's 6 feet 9 inches tall so they're going to be bigger – but even compared with someone of the same size his lungs are larger, enabling him to process more oxygen which in turn allows him to be more mercurial, to punch like a heavyweight but dance like a middleweight even into the twelfth round. But for all that, if he doesn't train and put the work in, this physiological bonus amounts to nothing.

The idea that a person can reach the very top of their chosen profession by sheer force of their own will is also a myth; it's never just one person but a set of circumstances and key people that help you on your way. Look at Mike Tyson, former World Champion and Olympian. Without the life lessons and direction of his coach, Cus D'Amato, Tyson would have probably remained a street punk and career criminal and would probably be dead by now. But D'Amato, who had coached José Torres and Floyd Patterson, channelled Tyson's hoodlum energy and gave him an outlet for his anger: the ring. Between them they created Iron Mike, the deadliest, most brutal boxer since Sonny Liston. At the age of eighteen, the same age as me when I won my first Olympic gold, Tyson became the youngest ever heavyweight boxing champion of the world. When the elderly D'Amato died, Tyson soon went off the rails and ended up in prison, his best boxing days behind him. There's no one factor that contributes to greatness but many. And when you take away one of the foundations the whole Jenga tower comes tumbling down.

Matthew Syed retells the story of Anders Ericsson, a psychologist at Florida State University who in 1991 conducted an extensive investigation into the causes of outstanding performances. The test subjects, violinists at the Music Academy of West Berlin, were divided into three groups: the first group were outstanding students, the second group were good, while the final group were the least capable. The most significant factor between the best and worst musicians, they discovered, was how much practice they had put in. The best violinists had, by the time they were twenty, practised an average of ten thousand hours, compared with the lower group's average of four thousand hours. Purposeful practice was the only factor distinguishing the best from the rest.

At the time of writing, the world of boxing is salivating over a long overdue fight between world heavyweight boxing champions Anthony Joshua and Tyson Fury. Tyson Fury is known to say: 'Styles make fights,' and these are two very different fighters. Fury, now thirty-one years old, is the more experienced with a higher ring IQ thanks to boxing running in his family: his uncle Huey trained Tyson in his gym from around the age of fourteen, his uncle Peter took over and guided him to his first world title, while his father was also a professional boxer, so he grew up in a boxing environment. Joshua, though an Olympic gold medallist, is by contrast much less seasoned and didn't grow up in a household where the sport was a passion. The same age as Fury, he didn't take up the sport until 2007 when he was eighteen. So, in terms of time spent learning ring craft, Fury has *at least* four thousand hours more knowledge than his opponent. This will tell in ring resilience – Fury is used to going twelve rounds and knows how to pace himself through the low points.

Just to add further spice to this story, since I first started writing this, the dethroned ex-WBC champion, Deontay Wilder, has now won his right for the third bout he and Fury signed a contract for to take place. After beating the then ruling heavyweight world champion, Wladimir Klitschko, in 2015, Tyson Fury dramatically fell into a pit of drug-addled, alcohol-soaked despair, his 6 feet 9 inch frame ballooning from 18 and a half stone to almost 30 stone. Fortunately, he had an epiphany moment in a bar one Halloween night; dressed in a skeleton suit, his stomach bulging from it, drinking pints with his mask on so people couldn't see his face, he caught sight of his reflection and felt ashamed. That night, on his knees, he asked God for help. There was another epiphany when he was behind the wheel of his Ferrari racing at high speed towards a concrete bridge with the sole intent of killing himself. At the last moment a voice inside him asked whether he wanted to leave his children without a father. He screeched to a halt on the hard shoulder a few feet short of his solid target.

What followed is one of boxing's great tales. Within eighteen months 'the Gypsy King' got a hold of his demons, lost the pounds, slimming down to a muscled 18 and a half stone, regained his license to box, and then in December 2018 achieved a draw against the world champion and most feared knockout merchant in history, Deontay Wilder – despite being felled by his infamous killer punch in the twelfth and final round. Up until this fight none of the victims of the 'Bronze Bomber' had ever got up off the canvas within the count, but Fury opened his eyes and did the impossible: like a pugilistic Lazarus he climbed to his feet and finished the round on top. In February 2020 he faced Wilder again and won the WBC belt within seven rounds, becoming the new world champ. Nothing is impossible if you really want it, and no one proves this point better than Tyson Fury. His reason for going off the rails when he had finally realised his life's dream, to become the heavyweight champion of the world? Purpose. He hadn't planned what to do next.

I believe that in life we write our own destiny and can achieve whatever we set our mind to. I also believe that if certain key elements are present, they will help us reach our goal. I think the butterfly effect, the idea that small actions can influence massive results, is true in so far as it's the little things you do in your training and the way you approach it that later amounts to winning gold medals. For all you might practise, it needs to be married with talent and alloyed to sheer force of will if you are to enter the history books . . . and remain in them!

Step 9: Start a gratitude and self-observation diary

I've been keeping a diary for a while now and it's a great way of getting stuff out of your system, as well as creating a habit of being grateful for the positive things in your life. When we sit down and write about an issue, we are often much closer to finding a solution as we slow our thoughts down and focus. It doesn't have to take any longer than twenty minutes at the start or end of your day.

Chapter Ten

Separating the Athlete from the Person and Finding the Balance

The Olympic Rings in the dining hall at the Rio 2016 Olympics.
A day or two after my individual.

I've always seen myself as a bit of a split personality: one is a home bird who likes to relax, the other a person who has to go out and perform every day. That latter person is so competitive and amped up he's unpleasant to be around, and being him can be tiring too. Competitive Adam is so focused that he thinks of nothing else but improving and winning. Sometimes before a competition I used to be so wired I couldn't sleep as too much adrenaline was running through me. I remember one occasion I was racing in Manchester and I didn't get to sleep till 4 a.m. the night before. I told myself I was fine, went through my preparations and raced as normal. While the gladiator mindset is one that will push through all barriers with no excuses, the Manchester situation was not healthy – you need your sleep. It was a prime example of letting the athlete out of his cage too freely, so he took over.

In the training environment I'm known for the extremely high standards I hold myself to and expect my teammates to be at too. This can sometimes lead to conflicts in such a high-performance climate. In the past it really made my blood boil if others weren't pushing themselves as hard as me, these days I've mellowed a bit and am much more balanced.

'The Swimmer' me is at his best when he's fired up and shooting testosterone around his frame just before a race, or when he's pumping weights in the gym or beasting it in the pool. But the trick, I have learnt, is to always leave him behind so he can't come home with me.

Separating the competitor and the person

Separating your athlete from yourself allows you mental peace and clear boundaries. After losing the Commonwealth Games 50m race in 2018 I asked myself: 'What is my character feeling and what is The Swimmer feeling?' From my *character's* perspective, I was happy for Cameron and told myself, 'It's just sport and he swam better than me on the day.' From the *athlete's* perspective, I wasn't happy, my anger was firing and I wanted to punch someone. I channelled that dissatisfaction as fuel for the fire of my purpose and came back a few months later to beat the world record. Defeat is good for you; it creates humility and you become a more rounded person from the experience of losing. It was the best thing that could happen.

If I hadn't developed this separation between character and athlete I would never be able to switch off.

I've become more in touch with my emotions since becoming a dad and it's made me better at being an observer of my thoughts and feelings and understanding how I work. I like to decompress after swimming through driving or walking. I'll think about work, process it, and then leave it completely behind before I go through my front door. I consider myself a veteran of the sport now as I've been doing it for so long and have been through so many ups and downs.

Keeping a diary every day is a great positivity barometer; the words on the screen are a direct litmus test of how I'm feeling in myself. Aside from how I'm feeling, I write about nutrition, how training went, what's working and what is not. It's about sharpening the sword of self-awareness so you can then make the necessary changes towards improvement.

All work and no play makes Adam a dull boy

Achieving equilibrium between rest and work and knowing when to push yourself hard and when to relax is critical to creating and sustaining success. Too much of one and not enough of the other is no good. You need to be able to switch off from your work so it doesn't completely possess you. Finding a balance between the all-consuming demands of being a pro swimmer and a family man is vital. In the best interests of those closest to me, my athlete – we shall henceforth call him The Swimmer – must be left at the pool after every session or championship. By keeping him separate from me if I have a bad day or race, I won't take it out on myself or the people around me. The selfishness involved with being a high-performance athlete is such that you must blank out everything else other than the challenge, the competition that lies ahead. It's like having tunnel vision. As a professional athlete there's only so long that my body will be capable of doing this and I am acutely aware of that. Friendships and family ties can break down when I'm in the super-focus zone, as I don't often reach out, call, text or come round in the evening. I just want to switch off with my boy and partner Eiri. Some of the closest people to me take it personally and despite my reassurances that I really do care, they think that I've changed through success and as a result I am ashamed of them and that I should spend more time with them. Sometimes it can appear as if I lack empathy or sympathy which isn't the case, it's just the super-focus of a selfish athlete kicking in. I'm not sorry for who I am, but sometimes I wish I could shape time as easily as I shape water; that way I could do everything that I need to.

If in doubt go for a walk

I look forward to going shopping at the weekend and doing fun things with my girlfriend and baby son. Sunday is my rest day. I love the British countryside, and before I race I use it to my advantage considering eventualities that might challenge me; the Stoic approach. I live on a hill and from its summit you can look out across the green hills rolling in mellow waves. It kind of resets me mentally and spiritually and puts things back in their correct perspective. I think we are so much happier when we are in nature, it's as if we are plugging back into our essence. One of the ways you can evoke that feeling of self-awareness is to stop, take a breath and think about nothing apart from how you are feeling in that moment. What does the air remind you of, how does the wind feel on your cheeks? Be completely honest and present with your thoughts and feelings. As I write you can smell the summer in the air, literally taste it – the flowers in bloom, the sunlight lengthening. If you can, I recommend switching off your phone for thirty minutes a day and finding a piece of nature in which to just *be*. After all, this is where we come from.

When I was in Tokyo in 2019 for a holding camp before we flew to South Korea, one of the first things I noticed was that you could barely see a green space. I felt my mood dipping in the neon forests of alien written signs and high-rise concrete structures, but then to my relief, I found a leafy temple in the centre of the city and I could feel it feeding my spirit. There's the relentless pace of the city, the rat race speed – and there's a speed of you. Have you ever noticed that when you first walk across a field or into some woods you are moving with the pace of someone in a hurry, as if you're rushing to get somewhere, hurrying from one place to the next without being mindful of what you're doing? That's the speed of life. Your real pace is much slower and more in tune with its natural surroundings. Nature doesn't have a deadline to meet.

Cameron van der Burgh now works in the high-pressure world of finance and recently said in an interview with *City A.M.*: 'Sometimes you'll be having a bad day. I'll step off my desk and five seconds later I'm in the living room with my wife. You're not physically there because you're thinking about something else. I've now decided that when I switch off, I switch off. I put the computer away. And then my wife and I go for a 30-minute walk. That period allows me to ... distinguish what's work and what's play.'

I have a great respect for nature and how it heals us. It's in our DNA to feel better when we immerse ourselves in the presence of trees as it's where we as a species spent most of our evolution. In a very primeval way nature slows our pulse to a healthier, more sedate speed. Nature immersion, a fancy term for going for a walk somewhere green, resets the low-level stress mode many of us constantly operate in because of the demands of modern-day life. It gives me an endorphin rush when I'm walking and having conversations with good people. If things don't go as well as planned in my day, I know I can always rely on nature to earth me back to normal and improve my perspective.

Train hard, fight easy

When you've trained hard, you can fight easy. I see the Olympics as a kind of promotion – I've got 56 seconds to focus in order to earn it. I know I've worked as hard as I can. I don't give myself the excuse to let up, though I do respect what the Royal Marines refer to as 'tactical withdrawal' if I am feeling off. A lot of athletes don't realise the value of a good rest – both mental and physical. It can give you a second wind when you most need it. The number of elite athletes who struggle with mental health is surprisingly high. Even some of swimming's legends like Michael Phelps, Ian Thorpe and Allison Schmitt, who have fifty Olympic golds between them, were not immune to it. Recently, at the Tokyo Olympics we had a number of athletes who spoke up about their mental health and achieving the difficult balance between the relentless pursuit of excellence and taking care of self. I too have experienced depression, especially after losing to Cameron van der Burgh at the Commonwealth Games in 2018. It was towards the end of the year and I didn't have any races. Because it was off-season it allowed me to party and I was drinking a lot. I'm a performer, and if I don't have something to perform at, I derail. It didn't last long and I tired of burning the candle at both ends. I must have been pissed off at losing as in 2019 I came back to break my world record with a sub-57.

I think for many sportspeople the only way to find gratification is through achievement, because who else would work 99 per cent of the time in absolute agony and train for an event which – in my case – lasts 56 seconds? Achievement doesn't guarantee happiness, and it took a while for me to recognise what's important and what's not. Breaking world records is no less appealing to me but there's a bigger picture for me now; after work I go back home and cuddle my boy, George, and that gives me immense joy. That's my happiness – creating an environment for him where he can push himself to the limits and learn more about himself. I've got to a point in my life where I can disconnect from swimming – it's not the only thing that I live and breathe now. When George was born, I was overcome with love. It's hard to describe just how powerful an emotion it is. And it has changed me and my priorities: I no longer care if I'm tired and beaten up by training, or if someone else has swum a quicker time, because every night I can let go of all that and lose myself in my new family.

Before George, my mindset selfishly orbited around the single goal of being the most dominant swimmer the world has ever known, but it is no longer so me-centric; I'm doing it for Eiri and George now – they are my inspiration. I want to be a good role model for him and a great dad. That's not to say I'm no longer as obsessed when I am in work mode, and sometimes it upsets people who don't know just how busy my day is.

I think we all put pressure on ourselves to get a better job and higher salary. I suppose that's a culture we've created, but it's not healthy. Sometimes it's not a bad thing to just pause and look back at your journey and say: 'Bloody hell,

I've come this far!' Researchers estimate that in 2016 around 745,000 people died worldwide of strokes and heart disease related to overworking – fifty-five hours as opposed to the prescribed forty hours. It's a 30 per cent increase since 2000. And with Covid-19 making people redundant and those who have survived being culled taking up their slack – as well as doing their own work while operating from home – the figure is only going to jump even higher. According to the World Health Organization, 'Working 55 hours or more per week is a serious health hazard. It's time that all governments, employers and employees wake up to the fact that long working hours can lead to premature death.' The lines between work and home have become blurred in the very place that should be your sanctuary.

We have to learn to manage ourselves and take care of our mind as well as our body. It's about finding the right perspective. I believe it is the small things in life that make it special, finding joy in what we do and enjoying the journey.

Enjoy the journey

I used to worry about myself, post-career – how I would deal with the reality that I won't ever have the high-octane life I'm having now. Learning to accept that is important. Matching my current life with an equally adrenaline-charged existence won't happen, so I need to get as much out of the *now* as possible and enjoy this part of my life's journey.

Enjoying the journey is about identifying the things that stop us doing just that; we get caught up in what's in the calendar today and next week, the bills coming in, the mortgage going out, and before we know it we are utterly divorced and separate from the present. We need to make sure our personal admin is efficient and up to scratch, getting all the boring, niggly stuff done quickly and efficiently so we can really soak up the present.

The fox and the swimmer

Recently I was lucky to chat with ex-SBS soldier and TV presenter Jason 'Foxy' Fox. We talked about a number of subjects, one of which was learning to live in the moment in order to feel most alive. Foxy tells a great story about the importance of staying present. Having found a doctor to treat his PTSD, a lady called Dr Alex, the two of them held their sessions on long walks they would take in the woods. Motion and nature go well together; that's when many of us have eureka moments. One day, on one such walk, they came across a mother and her daughter, who was probably no more than three. The little girl was kicking through leaves and puddles laughing with pure joy while her mum grumbled about how dirty her clothes were getting. Dr Alex said, 'Look at her. Children don't care about what's happened previously or what's happening in the future, they just care about the now, they follow their own feelings. They're not governed by anything. Why can't we all be like that? Well, we can ... You *can* be like that. You *are* like that.'

According to Foxy, 'You have to live in the moment. You can't do anything about the past, it's finished. And you can't deal with the future, you have to just live moment to moment, almost like a child would.'

Always keep singing

Know yourself well enough to notice your personal warning signs of low mood. I'm a naturally optimistic person and I can easily tell how bright my inner engine is burning because every morning I sing in the car as I drive to training. When I'm in a low mood I definitely don't sing, my energy shrinks and I'm more internalised, whereas when I'm feeling good, I notice all the colour and sounds. I also notice people more and meet their smiles with my own. When you're in a high state of energy your senses are heightened because your body wants to be stimulated and is open to it. One of the nicest smells is spring: the trees in leaf, flowers blooming, grass is being cut. It smells like hope.

During lockdown I hadn't had a conversation with many people outside of my own circles and I missed having fresh conversations with people I didn't know and who I could perhaps learn from. If we are to develop ourselves and widen our outlook, I think it's important that we seek out and expose ourselves to someone's else's journey and wisdom, for in doing so you enrich your own understanding of the world. I didn't have much interaction with many people even before the first lockdown because of my time and energy being my most finite resource. I really enjoy meeting people and swapping stories with each other. As a species this is one of our biggest strengths, the ability to save one another tribulations by generously shared wisdom.

Travel educates

I love Rome. I think it's my favourite city. In sport we are continually trying to improve, to use the arena to our advantage, and to race, fight and entertain people. Growing up I loved the Russell Crowe movie *Gladiator* and was obsessed with Roman legions, the various auxiliary groups, the Praetorian Guard, siege warfare . . . Ancient Rome was more of an idea than a place, a wonderful concept. For me the modern city is something similar. I can't put my finger on what exactly its greatness and appeal is – the food, culture, history and people, it's a mix of everything . . . I just know it is my favourite place.

Every time I race in Rome I try to visit the Colosseum and am always awestruck by it. *Now this is an arena!* I think to myself. When you come out in the swim arena and your name is called you hear a growing rumble in the crowd which builds to a deafening thunder, a colossal vibration, and you think, 'This is what I train for and this is what I live or die for.' Obviously, you don't die in the pool, but you have to leave every bit of yourself in that water, extract every ounce of effort from yourself.

Step 10: Meditation keeps you in the present

A meditation can be as simple as lying on your back, closing your eyes and feeling the breath run in and out of your body. Try a six-second inhalation followed by a six-second exhalation. Focus only on the breath, and when you become distracted by a train of negative thought, reject it and, without self-judgement, return to listening to your breathing. Ten minutes' meditation is a good place to start, working up to a meditation that lasts half an hour. There are lots of free guided meditations on YouTube.

Chapter Eleven

Following the Science – Diet and Exercise Tips

End of 2019. I spend a lot of time in this room!

Food has a direct influence on our energy levels and our health. By eating the right food at the right time, we fuel our bodies for optimum performance. This short chapter will give you an insight into what I eat to sustain myself through the day and the training that I do. Michael Phelps was renowned for putting away a lot of food, perhaps as much as 12,000 calories per day. Sport science has come on a lot since then; these days it's more about fuelling for performance rather than putting away 'X' amount of calories. It's also important that we focus on cleaner foods so we're not carrying excess body fat.

Physique

I'm a different shape to many swimmers because I focus on lifting weights, increasing strength and conditioning out of the pool, which builds more muscle. My body can pile on muscle very quickly, and if I'm not doing aerobic exercise which keeps me slim, I put on too much bulk. During the first lockdown, when we had no access to the pool for six weeks and I was working out in my garage, I went from 93 kilos to 103 kilos. Swimming is a great aerobic fat-burner if you swim 55,000 metres per week at a hard pace.

I love the gym, the raw power and strength. I'm in the water most of the time so it's a great contrast. I love lifting weights. I can bench-press 150 kilos, but I listen to the experts and don't forget about hydrodynamics. After all, what is the point of working out if it is slowing you down? Also, it's important not to push it too far, too quickly. The biggest threat to an athlete's career is injury. Although I always have the odd ache or niggle, I've never actually been injured, perhaps because I listen to my body very carefully and am in tune with it.

Rob, my gym coach, says I am an anomaly because I can push and achieve whatever he wants me to lift – despite the 55,000 metres a week that I swim – and then recover by the next day. Having a naturally speedy recovery is very helpful. I have a big skeletal frame that muscle can adapt and grow on quite quickly. When my physio rubs my back, she says it goes red very quickly which is the blood rushing to that area to heal it.

Diet

Over the last twelve months, under close supervision from my coach and dietician, I have been fasting. In a twenty-four-hour period I fast for fifteen hours from 9 p.m. till 12 p.m. the next day. You may wonder how I have the energy to train at an elite level the next morning for four hours? Firstly, it is about using the power of your mind and body. I'll be using the fat stores in my body which keeps me lean but also provides me with a constant source of fuel. Fasting has allowed me to up my training and I no longer get the morning fog brain after breakfast as no blood is having to rush to my stomach to digest anything. Nothing passes my lips apart from black coffee or water. If I have eaten well the night before, the surplus calories carry me through my fast the next morning. When I'm getting lean, I'm on 2,500 calories per day but if it's a particularly hard cycle of training I'm in I'll up it to 4,500 calories. In the morning, while still on my fast, I get better sessions because my body has gone into fat-burning mode. I used to have big meals before training and would feel too heavy. When we digest a big meal blood rushes to the stomach, whereas with fasting it goes straight to your brain and your muscles and you feel more energised.

If you cut your diet down too much you won't be producing enough testosterone. Your nutrition should change according to what you are doing. You need to know what you are eating and why. To maintain muscle mass and ensure that my levels of amino acids are high, I use sports nutrition supplements.

My daily diet

12 noon: Two fillets of white fish, two baked sweet potatoes, green beans, banana and salad (400 calories).

2.30 p.m.: Porridge (150 grams), fruit, protein shake and brown toast (950 calories).

5 p.m.:   Protein drink and protein bar (230 calories).

7 p.m.:   Sushi (750 calories).

8.30 p.m.: Protein shake and three slices of brown toast (300 calories).

Gym

There are eight key areas Rob, my long-time strength and conditioning coach, works on with me.

Compounds: horizontal press, vertical pull and bilateral lower body

These drills vary in content and focus, at times being used for endurance, strength or power. My cornerstones are squats, chins and bench press.

Rowing or horizontal pulling

Another compound-exercise type but utilised in every single session. It is used to offset the high volumes of work completed in the pool, promoting balance around the shoulder. Typically, this involves seated rows, machine rows, prone pulls and supine pull-ups.

Unilateral or single leg lower body drills

A focus for ensuring lower body balance. Cornerstone exercises include: split squats, reverse lunges, step-ups and sled work.

Posterior shoulder work

Same rationale and frequency as reported in rows. Exercise examples are: flys which, using dumbbells, focus on the chest pectorals and deltoids; hip pulls which, pulling a cable between the legs, concentrates the glutes and hamstrings; and sea turtles which improve core and strength, posture and increases the muscles protecting the scapula.

Hip conditioning work

Focused around ensuring resistance to common injury sustained by the demands of the pool. An increased focus on groin-work specific to the demands placed on this area in breaststroke swimming. Cornerstone exercises: adductor bridges and travelling side lunges.

Trunk conditioning

Evenly distributed between posterior (lower back), anterior and lateral aspects. Key drills: plank, skier crunches and high-reach sit-ups.

Thigh conditioning

This could be isolated quad or hamstring work. Cornerstone exercises: hamstring bridges and hamstring curls.

Long-lever shoulder work

Predominantly propulsive actions of swimming, via more specific, extended mechanics.

Gym workout

Clap press-ups

Three sets of five reps. Builds explosive power.

Barbell back squats

Three reps, five sets. Builds muscle in the quads, glutes, hamstrings and lower back which account for 70 per cent of the stroke's power.

Barbell bench press

Three reps, five sets. Helps build strength and power for that extra 30 per cent of my stroke. It's where you catch the water and most of your technique settles.

Chin-ups

Five reps, three sets. Builds back muscles, biceps, triceps and muscle in the forearms.

Extended crunch

Twenty reps, three to four sets. Strengthens core.

Supplements

Hydration tablets help replace electrolytes. In the pool you never know how much you are sweating so it's easy to become dehydrated. I have two of these tablets per day.

Between my two swim sessions each day, I have two protein shakes or bars and once a day I'll either take an overnight protein or a specific homemade protein smoothie. Supplements get too much credit for sporting performance and progression. The hint is in the name 'supplement'; if your main meals provide you with enough carbs, protein, fat, nutrients and minerals you shouldn't need many supplements. I try and take as little as I can but it's really hard for me to get as much protein as I need to recover in time. Use them sparingly in places where you can't eat a healthy meal.

Chapter Twelve

When the Pupil Is Ready the Teacher Appears – Mel and Me

January 2016. I spent 7 weeks out on the Gold Coast and this was a huge contributor to my success in August.

My coach Mel used to give me a lift to college in Derby, where I was studying, after our early morning pool sessions. It would be rush hour and – bless her – she was working two jobs at the time, and she hated the fact that by driving me she would pass her house on the way and then be snarled up in traffic afterwards. But the positive in taking me was that she could use this time to influence me with honest conversations about training, the Olympics, and dealing with nerves etc. Looking back on your life you realise the impact certain people have had. The most generous gift someone can give is their time, and Mel always makes time for people. I'm like a racing dog that needs stimulation and can't sit around unoccupied. I get itchy feet and need to be constantly doing something, which is a blessing and a curse.

What unites her and me is our work ethic and not being

afraid of the grind. I've always known that the harder I push myself, the bigger the payoff. I'm just wired like that. Mel used to say, 'Whoever is in my team needs an education to fall back on.' She cares a great deal about her swimmers. Amazingly, we are in our twelfth year of working together. I would never be where I am without her guidance and friendship. This is her take on me:

'I've weathered every storm of Adam's development. When you start coaching a young athlete you're very directive, but now I'm his belief partner. He comes to me for advice. I'm not manipulating him now but let's just say I'm controlling the orchestra from a different place. Adam is a very dominant character who likes to do things his way. The ego override has to be my decision; the way to influence him is to get to him before he is thinking about it, so I plant the seed with him and he thinks it's his idea!

'As the athlete gets older you as the coach have to evolve with them. We're a brilliant match, both competitive. The moment I saw him do breaststroke I thought, wow, this kid is a bit different! The biggest thing for Adam was the challenge of getting to him to access our training environment. I contacted his current coach and I met with his mum and dad. I told his mum, Caroline, that he had real talent. They're not an affluent family and it was a long way for him to go every morning – forty minutes each way – and it was going to be a stretch financially to get him to enter into what is a middle-class sport. How could we get him the training he needed to shine?

'His mum was very open to supporting him. I told her he needed to be at the pool for 5 a.m. and she said "What!?" I would help out where I could, creating opportunities for his mum to share the burden – like arranging a place to stay on Sunday evening before training, and picking him up myself some days. We started gradually building from one morning a week to six times per week.

'Someone asked me how it felt to see him grow into a world champion of such distinction. Winning at Rio was the biggest moment of relief for me. We'd been together eight years by then and I'd always believed he could do it, but there were so many battles I had to go through to protect him. I had people calling me a paedophile because I picked Adam for a team and another boy lost out, but I had a good feeling that he was going to be the quickest. While Adam was starting out on his journey and was enjoying the environment, behind the scenes I was suffering like hell from being bullied and accused of favouritism because I wanted the club to be successful. When Adam won at Rio it was a big "fuck you" to all those naysayers that didn't believe in us. It means such a lot to me that we proved them all wrong. I wanted to make great changes and stand up for the things I believed in, and I always had an unshakeable belief in Adam. People said our club was not going to produce any great swimmers, how wrong they were.

'The depths of our relationship and what we've been through is considerable: we've cycled through Africa together, I've taken him on training camps, and bought him his first car. I think Adam would call me if he needed advice or help. The programme I ran at the City of Derby club was supposed to send the good swimmers from our club to the Performance Squad down the road. I didn't believe in that – I just wanted to make my swimmers the best they could be and hold on to them. We started out with a small pool with just a few slots a week there, very little pool time. But I was full of energy and enthusiasm, and I'd just come out of elite sport, so I was probably the best mentor for that group of kids; I gave them everything that I'd missed out on myself as a professional athlete. We formed a community; I'd take them bowling, I wanted them to have fun.

'What raises Adam above his peers is his work ethic. It's a combination of devotion to his task and genuine talent that has made him the most dominant champion in the history of sport. You listen to the stories of the very best athletes, and they are the same, whatever the sport: David Beckham was always the last person left on the training field, while Jonny Wilkinson was always the first on it. Adam is like that. The difference between the good and the great is that the great love the grind – they look for it, they ask themselves how they *can suffer more and make it more difficult so they can conquer more. You don't get to be the best in the world without having talent, but you also need character, grind, work ethic and attention to detail. You need the right coach, family support, a place to train ... it's like an alignment of planets where everything falls into place. I believe it was fate for us to meet and work together. The three ingredients of our working relationship are: no bullshit, passion to work together – I'll do whatever I can to help him; finally, we both love winning and we like what comes with it and how you get to it.*

'Adam has been through the most gruelling physical challenges you can imagine. He can tolerate more than anyone else and he's a very quick responder. He has always responded to training exposure and that's one of his physical talents, that he can tolerate large amounts of workload capacity. That and size-12 feet and hands like spades!

'Adam's pre-Olympic routine – up at 6.45, then to the pool for his video check-ins, swim two hours. Then to the gym to lift weights, then home to George for a few hours, then physio, then two hours' swimming. He has the weekend off. It's all about balance; you can't make adaptations to the body if you don't allow it to fix, mend and recover, so it's crucial for him to be able to rest. With his age I now build the programme around how much he can recover, whereas when he was sixteen I looked at how much adaptation he could absorb.

'Adam has an ability to give an extra 10 per cent of commitment. When I first met him, he was an angry little kid. I told him that he needed to learn to use that anger sparingly and carefully – he didn't need to use it to get the last loaf of bread in the bread aisle against a ninety-year-old granny. It's where you place your anger that counts.

'We talked often about "Process Gladiator"; relinquishing desires in order to free your mind to deliver your best performance because you're so focused on how you do it. By sticking to this process, with the right emotional balance, you can summon rage arousal without getting arousal override to the point it inhibits your cognitive function.

'It's all right being heroic and diving into the fray blindly, but unless you're conscious of what is going on around you, you're going to be run down by a chariot or eaten by a lion. Pure red mist on its own is not helpful. Gladiators, if they were to have any longevity, had to have a fight plan and inner rage.

'Controlled aggression is about bottling your anger; it can be destructive, so knowing how to engage it is important, like letting an animal out of the cage – you can't let it out for too long because it will get tired and become ineffectual. You need to have the emotional intelligence of when, where and how to engage it. How to let the competitor run free without running amok. Imagine a boxer who fights with pure emotion: he's *going to throw lots of punches then eventually run out of juice as he punches himself out. He needs a fight plan and to pick his punches carefully. A Formula One driver knows not to drive around the clock at full speed with that passion in his belly – he has an emotion override which tells him to slow down at key moments.'*

In June 2021, Mel found herself on the Queen's birthday honours list and received a well-deserved MBE for services to sport and charity. It was the country's way of saying thank you to her for her tireless efforts to help myself and others fulfil their potential. The true measure of a good friendship is that it can weather change and evolve over time. Yes, we argue occasionally – who doesn't when you spend seven hours a day working together, and you are both super focused on winning? But we always bury the hatchet. The magic with Mel is how our relationship has changed over the years. As she explains: 'At the start of the journey you stand face on. Then it's more side leadership – you think together and make a decision. Now it's from the back. I'll be whispering what he needs to remember but he'll be telling me what else he needs. You become an advisor. He becomes the expert. He drives the car, I provide the information.'

Good coaches want the best for their athletes but great coaches find the best. Mel used the extensive network of swimmers and parents to drive me to and from training, when my mum couldn't find me a place to stay multiple times per week when it was 4a.m. starts the next day before college. For all those people who helped me from small tasks to large, know that I am truly grateful and each medal I win, know that a part of it is yours too.

Words fail me when I try and express how grateful I am to her, but I'll try. The Ancient Roman saying, 'He conquers who conquers himself,' sums it up perfectly; as without Mel I could never have channelled my energy and anger in such a formidably focused way, and for that I forever thank you, my friend.

Chapter Thirteen

Standing Up for What You Believe In

In 2017 I went back to Zambia to raise more money for Sport In Action.

Courage is not being afraid to put 100 per cent of yourself on the line and go for what you want, instead of being afraid to fail. It's about not being scared of your own potential. If we all found something we really cared about doing which also had a positive impact on those around us, the world would be a much happier place. It's better to have tried and failed than not to have tried at all. No regrets. We grow more through failure than success. Courage is also about standing up for what you feel is right.

Recently, I stuck my head above the parapet by supporting athletes' right to protest at the Olympics. In light of the Black Lives Matter movement, the International Olympic Committee has emphasised its long-standing ban on 'demonstration or political, religious or racial propaganda', be it on the podium, in the field of play or at the opening or closing ceremonies. A guest writer for *Swimming World* magazine was of the opinion that viewers watching the Olympics for some escapism from politics might feel alienated by protests. The view I expressed was that people should have the right to protest, and the right to do it where they want. I don't think they should be penalised for that. I've always had a certain view that the Olympics and sport in general shouldn't be political, but there are so many issues in the world, you don't want to take away the right of those athletes to protest. Many will be coming from countries and under government bodies who are rife with corruption, racism and inequality – don't these individuals deserve a voice?

On social media I wrote: 'Of course, Duncan Scott should have the opportunity to protest. If we all fall in line and never question anything these issues only get worse and the people causing them get even more power.'

We have to stand up and be counted for a number of reasons. For one, it helps you sleep better at night. Yes, I agree there is a time and a place to protest and obviously the Olympics need to run like clockwork and not get behind schedule, but sport is the most powerful vehicle for many athletes to be heard. If everyone you raced had been doping and somehow 100 per cent knew, you wouldn't stay silent. At the 2019 World Championships in Gwangju, my team-mate, Duncan Scott, refused to shake hands with Chinese freestyler and three-time Olympic champion, Sun Yang, following his drug ban in 2014. Good for Duncan.

There's an old saying, 'The standard you walk past is the standard you accept', meaning that if you know something is wrong but don't stand up against it, you are no better yourself. This might seem extreme, but look back at history and you'll see so many evils that were allowed to grow because people just sat on the fence. Black Lives Matter is not here by accident. Why are so many people thinking that it represents a threat to their civil rights? We've had enough institutional racism; I don't understand why we aren't all supporting BLM. It's important we educate our kids against racism and ignorance. I want George to know about colonialism and slavery as 25 per cent of his blood is Nigerian. Currently, there are so many instances of tokenism, people hashtagging BLM only to delete all these posts a few months down the line. Companies are big on this, trying to show they are empathetic by hastily putting black actors in adverts which represent their products, and TV programmes. If something threatens to affect their profit line, these huge corporations suddenly sit up and respond with knee-jerk support.

When we question why we are thinking or feeling something and have no logical explanation for it, then we need to get rid of it. I think this applies to racism. Since being with a partner who is half Nigerian, I have a deeper understanding of what white privilege can look like. Society is trapped in a loop of hatred. Why would we harbour hatred for someone of a different colour for no real reason save our own ignorance? There's a moment in the movie *American History X* where the main character, a neo-Nazi racist, is asked by a black man: 'Has anything you've done made your life better?' This is the moment the character turns and relinquishes his hatred. Racism is a two-headed snake that ultimately devours its vessel, the racist. It's empty, misspent energy.

Taking down all those statues of institutional racists certainly can't change the past; instead we must focus on the future and the present. I don't want George to look at history and say he hates his country; I want him to love his country as I do and for him to want to improve it from grassroots level in his corner of the world. We have to be the change – it starts with us. And we have to be better than we were yesterday. There's a wonderful quote attributed to an anonymous monk in the twelfth century:

When I was a young man, I wanted to change the world. I found it was difficult to change the world, so I tried to change my nation. When I found I couldn't change the nation, I began to focus on my town. I couldn't change the town and as an older man, I tried to change my family. Now I realise the only thing I can change is myself, and suddenly I realise that if long ago I had changed myself I could have made an impact on my family. My family and I could have made an impact on my town. Their impact could have changed the nation and I could indeed have changed the world.

First, we need to work on ourselves and then radiate the change, be the change. Set an example, lead by example. One person doing good things at the smallest level can eventually lead to meaningful change.

*

Sport has gifted me a wider view of the world. It has unlocked me physically and mentally. You get to learn about your foreign brothers and sisters and where they live. Going to Zambia a number of times was an amazing opportunity and it has given me a much wider perspective. You come back home and think, *Why was I even complaining about my life?* But then you very quickly slip back into taking your home comforts for granted, and the gift of free speech, and Zambia is suddenly a very distant place.

Sport in Action is a charity which gives support to kids in the developing world and also builds sport facilities in Zambian communities. These facilities foster teamwork and fair play through sport, and keep the kids off the street and out of trouble in a place where they feel safe. The first time we went to Zambia was in 2012, having raised around £35k. The next time we visited we raised around £30k. I remember one day we went to an orphanage where there weren't enough beds for the kids to sleep in, so we went to a local warehouse and out of our own pockets bought every bunk bed we could lay our hands on. It was the best money I'd spent in years. It's the girls who need the most help here as they are victimised and groomed for sex work at such a young age. Parents die of AIDS, and eleven-year-old boys find themselves in charge of the family. How can we expect them to have a balanced perspective?

When you look into a child's eyes, an orphan with AIDS, it's not a moment you forget. I want to travel the world with George from a young age, expose him to things so he can understand what the planet is about – even the bits none of us are proud of. I want him to meet the beautiful people of Africa, to take in the wildlife and its interesting cultures. I'll never forget the Zambian bike ride Mel and I did from Livingstone to Lusaka – no phones, no Wi-Fi, just being in the moment and having lots of conversations. Across Africa you see the darkest of human nature at work, but also the brightest and simplest and purest kind of happiness too.

I have such a lovely memory of playing basketball with some Zambian kids in 2017. They were gingerly coming up to the tattoo of a lion on my arm and touching it then running away. 'Mistah,' they said, wide-eyed, 'how did you get a lion on your arm!?' Then just as I was thinking how unique my lion was, a nine-year-old kid walked up and revealed he had a lion tat on his arm too! It makes me squirm a little when I think of the poverty in Africa in the same breath as the £70k I spent buying my first luxury sports car. But when you grow up in a poor household where the outgoings are more than the incomings, to be able to treat yourself to a brand-new, gun-grey Mercedes C-63 with all the mod cons is a moment to be savoured. I just pointed at it gleaming in the corner of the showroom and said: 'I'll have that one.' Although it's always worth checking what the insurance will be as a 21-year-old driving a V8. You really don't want to know how much I had to pay. I nearly fell over!

That was a while ago – a final act perhaps of me slaying that old ghost of financial insecurity. As I've got older, I've realised that while we all like nice new possessions – be it cars, clothes and holidays – the happiness they provide is fleeting and of little substance. The most important thing is putting a roof over your family's head. We live in a throw-away culture where if something is broken, we just replace it. Nowadays, I take pleasure in sitting down and fixing it myself, or at least the challenge of finding someone who can. I believe some of the happiest individuals I've ever met were those comfortable in their own skin. They didn't rely on props to make them feel or look better.

Diversity in swimming

When the American Simone Manuel won gold at the Rio 2016 Games, she became the first black woman to win an individual Olympic swimming event. Her achievement marked a watershed in popular opinion and unconscious bias, quashing the myth that black people don't make good swimmers because of their high muscle density. It was a great moment for diversity, but it's only the beginning of what needs to happen – nothing short of a culture change. My friend Michael Gunning used to swim for Great Britain and now represents Jamaica, and because he's black, when people see him out and about they always assume he's a runner – that shouldn't be the case. Marathon swimmer Alice Dearing is currently the only black swimmer who is part of Britain's elite programme.

Swimming is a white-based sport because culturally we don't reach out to black communities and get them involved in swimming lessons and make them feel included. I want to start to create that positive environment for people where no matter what race, age or background they are from they can be part of it. We have to identify a way to attract the nine- to twelve-year-old black kids and give them the opportunity to progress. Then it'll be a level playing field for everyone and it'll really be a simple matter of whoever is the fastest wins.

Role modelling

My son George has a Nigerian grandparent and my partner, Eiri, is half Nigerian, half Welsh. Having a son has given me more of an appreciation of the importance of leisure time and the magic of children. I feel and empathise more, especially with kids as they're the only innocent thing on this planet. Before I had a son, I didn't imagine how strong the connection was between a parent and their child, or what a powerful responsibility it brings with it. Kids act up based on how their parents act. They are sponges.

Back in the early 1960s, scientists at Stanford University conducted an important behavioural experiment in which seventy-two kids were divided up into three groups of twenty-four. Each group was separately shown into a room full of toys. In the first group an adult behaved aggressively towards a toy called a 'bobo doll', punching it or hitting it with a plastic hammer. In the second group the adult modelled gentle behaviour, while in the third group there was no adult whatsoever. Each child was then individually shown into the room of toys and left alone to their own devices. The results showed overwhelmingly that the kids who had observed the adult beating up the bobo doll tried to imitate this destructive behaviour, while those who weren't exposed were not aggressive. Kids soak everything up in their formative years and emulate the behaviour of their immediate environment. Having good role models is so important for their healthy development. My opinions and actions will trickle down to George.

Education

As I mentioned earlier, Mel Marshall has always insisted that her swimmers continue their education as a backup, but after I won at the Commonwealth Games and beat the world record in 2014, I decided I'd had enough of college. My tutors at Derby College were more than patient with my late arrivals – knowing that I had been up since before dawn in a pool, they had a rough idea of what I was trying to achieve.

Education in British schools is desperately in need of an update. I think we need to focus more on teaching our children emotional intelligence rather than spending six hours a day teaching something that they're not going to use in life. If we were to teach them how to listen to themselves maybe we would see less mental illness, depression and suicides.

We need to think more creatively about how we engage our children's minds. In Australia they now have schools which teach surfing from 9 a.m. to midday and then do the basics like maths, English and science in the afternoon. It's a good idea, as kids can express themselves physically and use up that restless energy in the morning so they are more settled in the afternoon to learn. These schools are appearing across the world. In Nottingham, where I live, there's a tennis school with the basic subjects and the rest of the time kids are playing tennis. I know we're living in different and hopefully more informed times, but I look back and think what the hell was I doing at eleven o'clock at night swotting up for a religious education test the next day?

In year eleven, I hated public speaking with a passion, probably as I had little confidence in myself. We'd have to get up and talk about ourselves. I didn't think my journey through life was going to be very inspiring or interesting to anyone. The career advice I was given seemed to confirm this. 'You're suited to being a builder.' No offence to builders – after all, my dad was one – but I disagreed. Thanks to swimming and seeing some immediate wins I grew in confidence and began to realise I didn't need to agree with someone else's opinion. Don't let anyone put you in a box and label you. Don't let them stunt your vision. We are here once and if you have an idea of something you want to try, then go for it. Ten thousand hours is a major investment, so make sure it is something you are really passionate about. I started a foundation course for a degree in sports science and lasted two months ... somehow, I knew I needed to completely throw myself into swimming. Life was too short to do something that didn't feed me.

Emotional control

Mental health is so important. Across the world, especially after the pandemic, there are tens of millions of kids living on the breadline without access to mental health therapy. Here in the UK, teens are falling by the wayside because the NHS, which I think is an amazing service, is too busy with Covid-19 to be able to offer appointments. Youths whose families are reeling from unemployment, whose schools were shut in lockdown, feel lost and forgotten and this anger is translated into violence and criminality. At school, instead of being schooled in emotional maturity we're still teaching theories that, to be fair, I forgot within a year.

Social media

We're living in an age where stress brought on by too much screen time on social networks and constant bad news on twenty-four-hour TV (which has us worrying about things beyond our control), has made us exist in the constant shadow of low-level anxiety. And now, as we begin to exit the pandemic, there's widespread high-level anxiety and hundreds of millions of people around the world in *flight* mode. As social media inevitably grows and becomes an intrinsic part of our lives, we're becoming even more unhappy. Real conversations – authentic, quality inter-actions – are becoming rarer. Is that really progress?

Social media was designed to connect people but it actu-ally disconnects us; people we used to talk to on the phone we now message instead. It also makes you feel discontented when you see someone else's life and start to question your existence. Social media is toxic narcissism and is a tool for capitalism, advertising and conspicuous consumption. It has wormed its way into our lives by giving us shots of dopamine every time we get a 'like' or a 'love heart' for something we have posted, maybe a photo of us on holiday, or with our family. Depending on the amount of good feedback we get we feel noticed, relevant and validated – or discarded, worthless and of little interest. And then there are those adverts that appear during our Facebook or Instagram grazing, with such uncanny precision that we think we must be being spied on or listened to by Alexa.

The dangers of social media

It's all too easy to get caught up with trying to outdo the Joneses. I'm able to separate from that and not get caught up in the status race. For me social media is my platform to inspire people and tell them they can have a good career in swimming. Instagram is smoke and mirrors: everything you see there, take with a pinch of salt. Social media can be a uniting glue but also a place of jealousy and negativity.

When I use Instagram to post a swim result or a photo of me and my family, I do so with a long stick and not without trepidation, as there are people out there who can't help but troll others and respond with envy and negativity. As you walk down the street passing strangers, you have no idea how much they might be suffering from mental or physical illness. Everybody has shit to deal with; we should bear that in mind rather than getting lost looking at photos of unreality, which is what social networking is all about.

Choose your battles wisely

Sometimes my critics say: 'It's just talent that's got Adam Peaty where he is – look how much he beats the others by.' I find that disrespectful, given the thousands of hours at the gym and the pool I've put myself through. I have to continually train my body and mind to reach the level I compete at and must go through the blood, sweat and tears like anybody else. But what is the point of losing valuable energy worrying about negative people? In life I've learnt that energy, both physical and mental, is not a limitless commodity and that it can either be wasted or put to good use. Remember the gladiators, the elite who trained regularly but fought only once or twice a year? They didn't fight unnecessary battles with the mob or get caught in a dialogue with them; they channelled their energy into preparing for those essential battles and did their talking in the sandy ring.

Faith in sport

We all have different lives and different paths set out for us – each of us has our own fate. And while I'm not religious and don't subscribe to an all-seeing god, I do believe we are interlinked with the universe and there is a cosmic energy at play. You get back what you put in. For example, a conversation with someone who is negative or positive will instantly impact on your mood. All it takes is something as little as a smile to be a catalyst to positive change. Energy is also a currency: you put in and take out when you need to. Religions and cultures dictate that we need a rest day in every week because we need to replenish that vital energy.

Funding

For swimmers starting out as professionals, I have to warn you, it's not going to be cheap. My first year of funding in 2012 from UK Sport was a lifeline and Mel literally had to beg for £3k for me. There are around six different levels of funding, starting at £3k. The London 2012 Olympic trials cost my mum two grand for the hotel bill alone for just one week.

To be a pro athlete in this country you need money. Pro swimmers need to pay for physios, nutritionists, supplements, suits and goggles; to even compete with the rest of the world you need a lot of financial support. These were the trials I went through in my early days before I was sponsored. To be the fastest I needed money to get there. I was very lucky to have had help from UK Sport who believed in me. Funding was a vital element in my success. I also had a lot of support from Sport England and the Rotary Club who donate money to athletes who would otherwise fly under the radar and whose talent wouldn't have the chance to grow. I haven't received APA (Athlete's Personal Allowance) since 2015 as I earnt over the threshold but I'm still supported in other ways, with access to elite training facilities, training camps and some of the best coaches in the world. Sport as a whole is grossly underfunded in comparison to the value it puts back into society and the economy. We need so much more investment into the grassroots of the sport and this is an issue I will try and tackle head-on. Who knows where the next Olympic champion will come from?

Over and out

It's been fun writing this little book over the last twelve months, a time in which the world has changed forever. I hope some of it is useful to you. I hope too there were moments that inspired you. Most of all I would like to think you will apply some of the lessons I've learnt to your own life. Time is so precious – don't let it run through your fingers. As I write this last page I am in my little room in the Olympic village and there is a brand-new gold medal on my desk that makes me grin every time I look at it. I wrote this on Twitter after my race: 'For my country, my son and my family. For those who stayed up through the night to watch me. For all those people who need a bit of light. You can get through this.'

Epilogue

Defence of My Realm

A few days after my son George-Anderson was born.
Moments I will cherish forever.

Though the Japanese have created a wonderful set-up for the Games, it couldn't be any more different to the effervescent, carnival atmosphere of Rio. I'm a show-boater, I feed off the crowd and recycle the pressure of their expectant cheers into my performance. I haven't raced for so long because of the pandemic, but thankfully with each of my heats the race rust has fallen away and my times have steadily improved. Imagine being in the cup final without having played any games during the season – this is what it feels like.

During the heats I've also been getting my head around the fact there are no people in the audience. I've been in livelier graveyards than this silent disco. Maybe a few hundred cardboard cut-outs of make-believe spectators peppered around the 15,000-capacity Tokyo Aquatic Centre would have given it some kind of atmosphere, but instead there's something eerily quiet about the place; it's as empty as a Japanese *shinto* (tomb).

Because the pandemic is still raging beyond the perimeter

of the Olympic village, no one has been able to get out and see Tokyo between race days. No matter, I've seen the city before and I'm not here to sightsee. I've come for the scalp of whoever is going to challenge me. Before Dutchman Arno Kamminga swam 57.92 seconds at the Netherlands trials earlier this year, I had the twenty fastest times in history. He's upset the symmetry and I'm not happy about that – time to knock him off the board, or maybe knock him out. According to an interview four weeks ago in Rome, he thinks he will take me on the second lap . . . maybe it will be his scalp I take back in my bag.

I'm not really troubled by Kamminga or the fact that he again clocked a sub-58 seconds in the heats, he's still a long way behind me. 'Times don't matter now,' Mel reminded me earlier that morning, 'it's just about winning the gold medal. No one remembers the time unless it's a new world record. They are more bothered about who wins the gold.'

I hear my name called for the men's final of the 100m breaststroke, stop pacing the ready room and strut to lane 4, the same lane in which I won my first gold at Rio '16. It's just where I want to be – in the middle of the pack. Thankfully, today there *are* a few souls in the audience with Union Jack flags, but it hardly feels like an Olympic final. Apparently it's the quickest line-up for this event in history, and victory will see me join the legendary Kosuke Kitajima of Japan, the only swimmer to have won gold in the 100m breaststroke at two consecutive Olympics – first in Athens '04 and then in Beijing '08.

We've been racing in the evening so far, but to accommodate American viewers all the finals are in the morning. That's a shame as everyone's times are slightly slower in the morning having woken up early. But last night I slept like a baby and woke this morning feeling renewed and ready to fight. I loosened off on a gym bike then ate a bowl of porridge and honey, and a banana in the canteen (which is about the size of four football pitches!).

A true champ knows that no one has trained harder than them, because they've given it everything. And some. A true champ is ready for whatever is thrown at them. I feel good, at home in my skin and, like Alexander of Macedonia, I'm ready to lead the team from the front. A true leader is undistinguishable from the rest of his troops; they don't need to tell people what they should do, they lead by example.

Around £20m has been injected into British swimming in preparation for these Olympics, and the coaches know they need to deliver. There's been a palpable tension in the Team GB camp all week and I feel a certain unspoken pressure on my shoulders to win the first British gold medal at the Games and open the door for other British athletes to follow. If they see me win, hopefully they'll say, 'We want a piece of the pie too.' But it's not just pressure from the team I feel burdened with, there are a lot of other things at stake: commercial deals and bonuses, not to mention my pedigree and pride.

I haven't trained for the last five years to go back to my country empty-handed. I've sacrificed my life for this sport, clocking up around forty hours' training per week, and I don't do it just for the love of the swimming; it's also about creating a financial cushion for those that I love. Plus, a lot of people rely on me to feed their families, never mind me feeding my own. It doesn't get more real than that. Everything is riding on the next *minute*.

Thinking of this I feel the burn in my chest, my temples pulsing and the sinews in my arms tense and untense, the mythic figures illustrated on them shifting impatiently. I breathe deeply and calmly, tempering the rage I'm summoning from that dark place, the primal cave from which heroes find the mettle required to be at their best. I'm racing between Arno Kamminga and Nicolo Martinenghi. They're both great, talented swimmers but neither will match me today. Just before I climb on the blocks I turn to my left and regard Kamminga in the lane beside me. I'm so focused on the race ahead that the face-off lasts less than three seconds. My lion tat is roaring at him, while the new Spartan soldier on my other arm is up for a fucking good scrap. 'You'll have to wait, I was here first!' thunders Achilles from my forearm. Then Poseidon calls my attention to the awaiting water stretching into the distance. And then the whistle blows for us to climb onto our blocks. Athena wisely works her magic and returns my mind to the process, which creates calm in the chaos.

As the bleeper shrieks I catch an explosive start. As I

knife into the cobalt blue it's as if my limbs breathe a sigh of relief. Pure silence greets me as I ascend from my underwater pull and I forget about those either side of me, especially Kamminga, quickly finding my flow. As I touch the wall at the turn I'm leading and just a tenth of a second from my world record. Then I turn it up a notch and give it full throttle. My lungs are working overtime, blood is rushing around my body as the turbo kicks in. I start to pull away from the competition and I'm in that special place of immortals for the briefest of moments. I feel as if I could keep swimming forever but the wall rushes to meet me and I glide in to touch it. The fury is still burning inside me as I look over at Kamminga who's come second. I fist-pump him. 'Come on!' I yell to the empty arena. It's a war cry to the rest of Team GB. I have won and the pressure is finally lifted after five years' preparation.

I don't care that I didn't break my world record – I am the first British swimmer ever to defend their Olympic gold medal. Pandemic, cancellation of the Games, moving house and having a child all in the same year – any one of these could have derailed me. People said being a new father would get in the way but I proved them wrong; it only made me want to fight harder. I can look George in the eye and say, 'All that time that I had to go training and leave you, and your mum, it was all worth it.' I know my beautiful partner and little boy are there for me whether I win or lose, and that means everything. This victory isn't all mine, but belongs to the British swim team, my family, friends and all those people I've had to put to the sidelines as I knew it was going to take every bit of energy to get to Japan and win.

Belief is one of those things that if you can visualise it, you can achieve it. If you can think it, you can do it. Me and Mel always say, 'Let's just get that plane flying.' But to get that plane flying you've got to build the plane, build a runway, do all the logistics, put the fuel in. There's a huge amount of effort that goes in, not only from Team GB but British Swimming, every single day – every single minute of every day. And that's why you get the performances you do. It's a huge commitment. In my case we're looking at thirteen, nearly fourteen years of extreme hard work. I'm the first British swimmer to ever defend an Olympic title, so I can wear that medal with a huge amount of pride. But I also know that I am leading a new generation of swimmers, and hopefully they can convert this triumph back home to inspire the grassroots level of the sport, which is what the Olympics is all about. It's my third Olympic gold, plus two Olympic silvers. It's incredible where you can go if you put your mind to it. Don't set a limit in the sky, always push. When you think you haven't got anything left, you've always got something. You'll always find a way if you want it enough.

Adam Peaty

England, August 2021

Bibliography

Meditations, Marcus Aurelius, Macmillan, 2020

Pathways to Bliss, Joseph Campbell, New World Library, 2004

Papillon, Henri Charrière, Robert Laffont, 1969

Flow: The Psychology of Optimal Experience, Mihaly Csikszentmihalyi, Rider, 2002

You Are the Placebo: Making Your Mind Matter, Joe Dispenza, Hay House UK, 2014

The World's Fittest Book, Ross Edgley, Sphere, 2018

Battle Scars, Jason Fox, Transworld, 2019

Outliers, Malcolm Gladwell, Penguin, 2009

Can't Hurt Me, David Goggins, Lioncrest Publishing, 2018

First Man In, Ant Middleton, Harper Collins, 2018

Human, All Too Human, Friedrich Nietszche, Penguin Classics, 1994

Thus Spoke Zarathustra, Friedrich Nietzsche, Penguin Classics, 1974

Break Point, Ollie Ollerton, Blink, 2019

The 5 Second Rule, Mel Robbins, Post Hill Press, 2017

The Little Prince, Antoine de Saint-Exupéry,
    Reynal & Hitchcock, 1943

The Stress of Life, Hans Selye, McGraw-Hill, 1956

Letters from a Stoic, Seneca, Penguin Classics, 2004

Start with Why, Simon Sinek, Penguin, 2011

Bounce: The Myth of Talent and Power of Practice,
    Matthew Syed, Fourth Estate, 2011

A Return to Love, Marianne Williamson, Harper Collins,
    1992

With Mel in Tokyo. Exhausted but also so relieved at having defended my 100m Olympic Champion title.

Top Tunes

My top tunes for getting plugged into rage . . .

1 'And I Will Kiss' – Underworld (memories from London 2012)

2 'Purpose' – Potter Payper

3 'Unwritten Bars' – Ard Adz

4 'Same S**t Different Day' – Skepta

5 'Trenches' – Tiny Boost

6 'Turn the Page' – The Streets

7 'Gone With The Wind' – Architects

8 'Buggin' – Hot Since 82

9 'My Head Is A Jungle' – Wankelmut & Emma Louise (MK Remix)

10 'Phantom Fear' – Architects

. . . and for calming down again.

1   'T.F.T.T.I.' – Euroz

2   'Teenage Fever' – Drake

3   'Love Galore' – SZA feat. Travis Scott

4   'Patient' – Post Malone

5   'On Your Own' – Jorja Smith

6   'SAD!' – XXXTentacion

7   'I Don't Wanna' – Adje

8   'Days in the East' – Drake

9   'Needed Me' – Rihanna

10 'It Runs Through Me' – Tom Misch feat. De La Soul

Acknowledgements

I'd like to thank my mum and dad, Caroline and Mark, for instilling in me the values I live by and for dedicating their lives to guiding me through mine.

Thank you to Mel Marshall, my mentor and coach, who has been by my side throughout and has shown me you can still smile through adversity even when things get tough. Thank you for guiding me through the darkness when there was no light to be seen.

Thank you to Ed Baxter, my friend and business partner, for committing his life to developing and helping the next generation of swimmers.

Thank you to all my closest friends who've had an enormous impact on who I am – you know who you are.

Thank you to Rob Woodhouse for having a clear vision from day one and helping me navigate rough waters.

Thank you to all the people behind the scenes who have made an impact, big and small – the many volunteers, coaches, timekeepers, venue staff. And thank you to everyone who has supported me on my journey - hopefully this book will inspire you on yours.

Thank you to my publishers, Quercus, and everyone involved in making this book a reality.

Finally, thank you Eiri for raising our son George with all your love and warmth.